IN LIGHT OF GENESIS

JEWISH POETRY SERIES
Yehuda Amichai / Allen Mandelbaum   GENERAL EDITORS

Pamela White Hadas
IN LIGHT OF GENESIS

Else Lasker-Schüler
HEBREW BALLADS AND OTHER POEMS

Avoth Yeshurun
THE SYRIAN-AFRICAN RIFT AND OTHER POEMS

Pamela White Hadas

IN LIGHT OF
GENESIS ⌁

The Jewish Publication Society of America · Philadelphia 5740/1980

JEWISH
POETRY
SERIES

Copyright ©1980 by Pamela White Hadas
All rights reserved   First edition
Manufactured in the United States of America

Library of Congress Cataloging in Publication Data
Hadas, Pamela White.
    In light of Genesis.
    (Jewish poetry series)
    1. Women, Jewish—Poetry. I. Title.
II. Series.
PS3558.A311598I5   811'.54   80-13129
ISBN 0-8276-0177-8
ISBN 0-8276-0178-6 (pbk.)

Designed by Adrianne Onderdonk Dudden

For David, who has shed light on the darkest passages

Contents

Preface

The women who speak in this volume may not be, in a strict sense, Jewish women. Lilith is a temptress of Jewish men, a threat to family life, and a genius of disorder. Sarah was born to a family of idol-worshipers and just happened to marry a crazy man (also incidentally a member of this family) who needed to smash the idols of both their fathers in order to invent a new religious expression that was to become Judaism. Perhaps she was the first convert, but in what exactly did her conversion consist? Her marriage to Abraham? Her motherhood? Her final personal relationship to haShem? Rahel Levin was born to a Jewish family in 1771, in Berlin, and was brought up speaking Yiddish; nevertheless, her relationship to her family's faith is at best ambiguous. She bemoaned it, ignored it, and denied it by behavior, by marriage, and finally by baptism. Yet in an important way it never left her. These women's lives are given their shape and definition by Jewish myth, Jewish texts and commentaries, and particular Jewish responses to history. The three of them together, in their widely separated origins or originalities, illustrate the imagination, ideals, and agonies of a people continually isolated or exiled from what is imagined to be, for each individual, a promised land. The anonymous astronomer portrayed in "Woman with Quasar" is no less a seeker than Lilith, Sarah, or Rahel, though she locates her special promise in the most distant phenomena of space. Looking outward, past all human myth, tradition, and history, she is motivated to discover what she can of the secrets of genesis. How is this universal light created, this personal light?

The question of identity, whether exiled or at the center, is perhaps the ruling question of these poems. The women all ask: "What am I?" "What am I worth?" "Where do I start?" "What am I to become?" All accustom themselves to departures in order to find their own elusive answers. For Lilith, departures—from all Law and any of her brief establishments—are the essence of her life. It is in her departures she manages to define herself, in opposition to the sacred limits she helps to define for her creators and subsequently refuses to obey. Being immortal, she will never find her final belonging. Sarah's departures—from land after land in search, and from her own common sense—are for the sake of her husband's fulfillment. She is a model of spirited acceptance and ultimate faith in Abraham's faith, despite the parts of it that may seem ridiculous to her at first. She finds her definition of herself in marriage, and only her death will find her in a place of her own. Rahel is, insofar as she is exiled from her origins by historical realities and prejudices, exiled from what she feels to be her essential self. Her inexhaustible questioning and self-conscious suffering are inevitable for her not only in the context of the Enlightenment, but in light of the inescapable circumstance of her Jewish birth. In the end she must admit the real and not inauspicious force of the latter in giving her her identity. The scientist is portrayed with the object of her investigation, identified with its elusiveness, framed by dedication and question.

Apart from identity and self-definition, to find secure belief in something Other is a difficult trial for all the characters of these poems. Lilith is imagined to have been created by God's own gasp of incredulity at His Creation. Sarah laughs, both appropriately and inappropriately, with incredulity, and names her son Isaac, after laughter. Rahel possesses the worst emptiness of incredulity and fills it with triviality and unconvincing suffering. Until she discovers what her real suffering consists of, hers is the saddest case. Yet all do come to acknowledge the Other, and to find themselves justified and identified by doing so.

The mythical, biblical, and historical concerns of Lilith, Sarah, and Rahel are overtly, covertly, and particularly Jewish, or so it seems to me. The woman astronomer is engaged in a quest that, although outside traditional religion, suggests to me similar mythopoeic possibilities and demands upon vision. In a larger sense, though, they are generally feminist and universal. To put it another way: all searching, suffering, and self-conscious (in both good and pejorative senses) people may be seen as metaphorically "Jewish." Italo Svevo has put it most simply: "It is life that makes one a Jew." Elie Wiesel (in Harry Cargas's *Conversations with Elie Wiesel*) elaborates, with a note of optimism: "At one point or another, every person becomes Jewish — the moment he becomes authentic he genuinely — though metaphorically — becomes Jewish. And every Jew is universal the moment he is genuine." And John Berryman, in an authentic moment that appeals to me in light of the genesis of my own poems, comments:

Exile is in our time like blood. Depend on
interior journeys taken anywhere.

("Roots," from *Henry's Fate*, Farrar, Straus & Giroux, 1977, p. 58)

It may seem strange to offer a bibliography to a book of poetry, yet as my muse is curious, I feel compelled to list some of the texts he has raided. For information about Lilith I relied most heavily on Raphael Patai's *The Hebrew Goddess* (Ktav Publishing House, New York, 1968), Louis Ginzberg's *The Legends of the Jews* (The Jewish Publication Society of America, Philadelphia, 1913), and *The Zohar* (The Soncino Press, London, 1956). For Sarah's poem, I consulted these same books, along with the *Encyclopedia of Biblical Interpretation* by Menahem M. Kasher, volumes II and III, *The Book of Formation or Sepher Yetzirah,* translated by Knut Stenring (William Rider and Sons, London, 1923), *Genesis: A Commentary* by Gerhard von Rad (Westminster Press, Philadelphia, 1961), Theodor Reik's *The Creation of Woman* (George Braziller, New York, 1960), Dorothy F. Zeligs's *Psychoanalysis and the Bible* (Bloch Publishing Co., New York, 1974), and Dan Greenburg's *How To Be a Jewish Mother* (Price, Stern, Sloan, Los Angeles, 1965). The only text that I used for "The Passion of Rahel Varnhagen" is Hannah Arendt's *Rahel Varnhagen: The Life of a Jewish Woman* (translated by Richard and Clara Winston, Harcourt Brace Jovanovich, New York, 1974). All of the epigraphs to the sonnets in this last sequence are taken from Arendt's quotations from Rahel's letters and diaries. I feel that Hannah Arendt is as much a part of this poem as her subject or my re-treatment of it. "Woman with Quasar" was inspired by a Physics. Department Colloquium at Washington University in St. Louis, where Professor Margaret Burbridge, one of the leading authorities on quasars,. presented her recent research. I cannot claim to have understood the particulars of her lecture, but I was moved to spend a good deal of time afterwards in the physics library, to try to satisfy my curiosity about her curiosity. My greatest debt of all, source-wise and other-wise, and with regard to all of the poems in this volume, is to my husband David; I could not have made the poems at all without his library, his knowledge of it, or his generous encouragement and conversation.

PWH
St. Louis, 1979

THE PASSION OF LILITH

for Judith Weissman

When Israel was exiled, the Shekinah too went into exile, and this is the nakedness of the Shekinah. And this nakedness is Lilith, the mother of a mixed multitude.

Zohar, 1

I & II: The Creation and *The Created:* Lilith was Adam's first wife according to Hebrew legend, and one may speculate as to how and when she came to be. The traditional way to treat a legend is to add to and / or combine previous speculations concerning it, and this is what I have done. I imagine that Lilith took her first elusive form before the creation of "man," literally by the inspiration of God, by His unpremeditated gasp, seeing for the first time the magnificence of the earthly dawn He had made. Lilith, therefore, as I see her, is not part of God's plan. He is unaware of her compression and development in His dark lung and is taken by surprise when she emerges at last. This happens with no ordinary exhalation of His, but at the close of the six days when He surveys His work and observes to Himself that not only is it good, but *very* good. Lilith is freed on the emphatic word *very*, not on the *good*, and it takes a long time—perhaps eternity—for the good to catch up with her. She is God's inadvertent or unconscious creation, and this is what separates her from man and frees her also from God's direct control. Her unorthodox creation is responsible for her very original disorderliness and her very disorderly originality. It is responsible for her mystery, her indignity, her special sort of passion, her burden and her gift.

I. *The Creation*

And when God saw the sea by light
He caught His breath...

II. *The Created*

Swept from the surface
trapped in unutterable black,
a star collapsed, reversed,
a diamond too deep depressed,
I thought I'd never come back
to be light and ease

until, with His last self-praise
riding astride the *very* not the *good*,
I rushed into the world, dishevelled, contraband,

neither hell-whelped nor heaven-pedigreed,
a creation preeminently
out of hand,
ready to finger the world, bitch, breed.

III. The Garden: God, not always above weariness and shortcuts, post-
pones the deliberate creation of a wife for Adam. He notices Lilith wan-
dering the world, His accidental and feminine by-product, and decides to
experiment. He puts His two sorts of creations—considered and inadvertent—into Eden together. Adam and Lilith, unfortunately but perhaps inevitably, do not hit it off. Adam would like Lilith to lie beneath
him in the sexual act, and to be subservient in every way; Lilith naturally
has other ideas. She leaves him and flies up to their great Lawyer in the sky
to petition for divorce, which God grants. She then, according to one account, proposes that God marry her Himself. As that is out of the question for Him, she sets out to make something of herself, and by herself,
on earth. She is the first liberated woman; in making new names for herself Lilith is merely her pseudonym; and though she leaves Adam's paradise without his particular curse, she manages very well to receive many
later on. This is her passion.

III. *The Garden*

On the other side from order,
the unintended bride,
one part gasp, one part express,
careless of symmetry, regardless of time...

What had the likes of me to do
with the likes of Adam?

Yet by after-whim
or black humor of Him
we were thrown together, clay
sun and glaze of moon—one
real garden with imaginary
goad—spitting image and spat upon—
Adam named and I with pseudonym:

man plus manifold, sure to explode
belief and make-believe
alike, alone.

Then Adam nearly drove me
mad—my original gaping
letter-man, docile as a stamp
and bland as logic,
flapping forever the divine right
of his real estate
at my obvious lack
of properties...

I tried at first to please,
opened my box of miracles for him;
he only wanted to hoe the peas.
He wanted his birds in his hand.
All mine gladly beat round the bush.
I wove an arbor, bindweed and angels' bane;
he wouldn't enter in.
He wouldn't lie under my crazy quilts
or improvise. He'd rather die.

              He had the Word,
had it from on high, while I,
previous to alphabets, superfluous as ampersand,
curled on chaos still, my edges blurred.

Gardens are made for orderers,
gardeners made to order,
but I am disorderable, the first trespasser.
So as Adam was carefully hedging his bêtes
and hugging the hedge,
and while angels were warring and setting
God's teeth on edge,
misfit and mislaid, I fled.

I gave a damn.
And I left my first love sucking
his green thumb.

IV. The Willow: Though Lilith chooses at first to live outside the stage where Adam's great drama will take place, she has been touched by him and his predicament. She would ultimately like to combine her free spirit with his bound humanity and this is the essence of her passionate mission. Legend has it that she hid in a willow tree directly after leaving Eden, mythical creatures above and below, and I imagine her using this shady and maternal place to develop her shady and maternal characteristics, to assess her position and prospects and the possibilities of her own invention. She must learn about the world no less than Adam, keep up with him in some sense for the sake of her self-respect as well as her curiosity. The willow is a traditional symbol of mourning, but it is also, for Lilith, a refuge and place of self-renewal. She tries to create offspring for herself the way the willow creates leaves, only to see them, like leaves, fall away. News of Eden and catastrophe is in the air and Lilith uses that to goad herself on, finally deciding that she has outgrown her first haven. Gentled somewhat, but still determined to make and break her own limitations, she exiles herself again.

IV. *The Willow*

At first it was creepy and wet and worse
than I'd thought to live at Eden's dispense,
dispossessed to learn alone the amiss
of a mass of wish,

to learn the way the willow grows,
find some shape in drift, small greens,
steal rain-secrets, wind-words, red sun
and weep, small wilts of light

> *while zu-bird over me and dragon under,*
> *silver and spotted cinnabar,*
> *guard my wonder.*

Willow within willow and all is hollow
as willow clairvoyance seeps through to me;
wormlike I weave the windborn news
from nonplussed Eden's Eve

into my tapestries of exclusion; wind laughs
to tell how bloodflesh blushes and writhes
to repeat itself. In secret meanwhile
I envy humanity, that far cry

> *while zu-bird over me and dragon under,*
> *winged and fanged, somnambular,*
> *dream my plunder.*

Half-there in hunger, small wilts of light
sip and drop away; short shrifts of wind
unwind where I tire of willow obbligatos,
her capriccios of slush: i-wish-i-wish-i-wish...

The willow makes her living mourning
living shadows and she means to lose me too.
It is time to let fall my copper hair,
move on. I travel light.

> *No zu-bird over me, no dragon under,*
> *the refuge and this exile's over.*
> *I must ask more.*

V. The Desert: Self-pity is not the least of any exile's characteristics, and
it is one of Lilith's first really human accomplishments. She realizes she
must not let herself go soft with it, however, and she chooses experience
in the desert to harden her. By this time Adam's kind has established its
fallen civilization, itself hardened by work and exile, but Lilith sees the
human ability to reproduce as compensation for their pain and she wants
to learn herself how to join and create out of her elusive body and random experience. She figures at the end of her desert exile that she is ready
to confront her most particular desire—to have again a direct mortal
contact and mortal children.

v. *The Desert*

Out of the woods.
Here's my hard light. Clean slate.
The vulture rings me gold.
The lion roars me blood.
Rocks mimic life in the heat-
palsied air, its terrible weddings.
Where I dance it's a panic,
the sun direct in my hair, blood jade.
All day the wind rubs its back in the dust
like a dispossessed genie, and distance
opens and opens like a wound
hardening the new crystal ball of my heart.

> *There is no pity in the desert.*

I grow havoc-wings and mordant feet,
scrabble with scarabs on their playground.
Invisible midwife to prophet's shrieks,
I stare down distance like stone Sekhmet,
riddle the hot sky's cinema.
Sandblast scours my sleep.
The camel humps higher at my jokes,
bites back a bitter laugh.

> *There is no pity in the desert,*
> *a spit in the eye, but it's not enough.*

Who wouldn't get sick of the vulture's claptrap,
sphinxtalk and the rest of it?
Here is where raw visions lie
in a scorch in the sand to dissolve by night.
Nothing lasts.
I'm sick of the indignity
of picking my wishbones alone,
watching them whiten in the sun like dung
while Babylon flourishes in its curse
and blooms with the cries of children.

There is no pity in the desert,
a spit in the eye, but it's not enough;
and sometimes I miss the willow's tears, I must admit.

I've had it with everyday angry summer.
I'll have a part in their mopish fall.
For better or for worse,
I'm coming out of exile:
it is time and time again.

There is no pity in the desert,
a spit in the eye but it's not enough;
and sometimes I miss the willow's tears. I must admit
the old error the new trial.

VI. Premeditation: Having decided to crash Adam's party, Lilith talks to herself (not, we may assume, without hoping that Adam is overhearing) about how things stand with her with respect to the humanity she intends to revisit.

VI. *Premeditation*

From alas to alias, chrysalis to open hand,
from milk-tooth to wisdom tooth, base to bias,
which of us, Adam or Lilith, keeps a promised land?
He let me leave, found Eve, and even Genesis
left me out,
but he couldn't forget
that in the first place, first spouse, there was
some tenderness.
I have no land of any sort. All I have is promises,
and I haven't been able to keep one yet.

A part of me left excalibured in the willow,
a part of me left crossing desert stars,
spelling emptiness, left out to be
charming for nothing,
the greatest part not yet
played out. It is up to me
to take something back,
to impend in the wind,
to redden and man my transparent heart.
For a dam I'd be,
no mad Amorpho, but for lack
of him; and but for lack
of me he might have escaped the snake
with its insinuous rhetoric;
tasting me
he would not have asked for Eve
or craved a tree.
Outside of the clock and outside of the field
I've lived a part of Adam
he couldn't see,
a phantom woman grown from a phantom
rib, my nerves still hooked
on his somehow and he
wonders where those sudden pangs come from.

I have little to offer but my very-ability.
Too many spirits are riding
my accidental airs.
Men call them demons, so I hear,
and I am blamed for being
prolific with pandemonia.
But I swear
upon all my tree-life and sun-life,
I'm still bare,
dismantled as wind and immaculate as grass,
with no arms to defend
or hold my spirits in.

I trail my resolutions behind me
like a fallen angel's wedding raiment,

a tearing ripple of sirocco.
I've packed my knowledge sublimed as dust
and all my bloodless rags.
I plan to launder them in the blood of Babel,
scatter moon sequins and go out on the town
arrayed at last for something final.

I have been dreaming
of men so long I know
that they have also dreamed of me so
I am going back or going forth
and I think I shall love the idiocies of mortality:
its children real as apples,
its ceremonies bursting like pomegranates,
its women laboring—I want to learn
the hang of that.

VII. Meditation: Bearing Culture: Lilith considers culture to be whatever
has helped one to grow: that it is a hard thing to bear and that its repre-
sentatives must be borne in exchange, with and for others. She compares
her own culture with that of "Adam"—his name standing for all his descendants—and asserts that the pain of both their cultures should bring
them back together.

VII.   *Meditation: Bearing Culture*

Culture, that difference of beginning
growing: Adam had it first in gardening;
Eve took it from there to her laboring.
They both worked hard at it, built Babylon.
And how have I done by comparison?

I too was cultured by circumstance,
beginning dispersed and lifted happenstance
into one great sea-gasp, hardened by chance,
secreted by myself round the fact I got away
from Eden without the curse. But blood-thirsty,

famished for form and accoucheur,
I had to make likeliness and loveliness all over—
my nerve of willow-sap, my hair
of sunset, my fat the thick dark,
my muscle wind, my bone sunlight—work

like Hell 'til my lips took shape from all
departures, my hullabaloo identical
with storm, inscrutable as the grit-cored pearl.
Cultured? Yes, sheen after sheen round-about
cultured by rejection, the pearl's unsprout—

able heart
cultured by fuss and mayhem
cultured by dare and earthen wear.

I am the niminy-piminy frisky frau
of the fire, the fire, the fire...

O Adam and O Eve, are we that different now?

VIII. Coming To / The Men: In becoming conscious of the work that is ahead of her, Lilith recounts her past and the attitudes "Adam" has seen fit to take toward her. One of his myths about her is that she comes to him at night, seducing him by dream and hallucination, that she is thus responsible for the embarrassment of his wet dreams and for his unfaithfulness to his wife. In her meditation Lilith reveals that she is indeed interested in "Adam" sexually, partly now because she wants so much to be made pregnant in a human manner, but that she also wants to reawaken in him the sense of her mysterious and lost beauty. She reminds him that Solomon once invoked her presence because he, of all men, recognized the supernatural wisdom and the humor in her crazy abandonment. Lilith wants, nevertheless and at last, to be taken seriously.

In the first place
        Adam forgot
Eden's lily pond and wild
lilies in the vale; having Eve
        Adam forgot himself
and in the second place
while he was counting begats and gold,
while he was stomping the marriage goblet,
while busy despoiling the alpha-omega,
scrolling and unscrolling the pentateuch
according to season...
        Adam forgot then
how one Lilith tried to give him a wilder balm,
how even in Eden I dressed to kill
in chrysoprase, beryl, lapis, opal...
thirty-nine jewels in all.
And now how easily might his offspring fall
into long gentle sighs toward me as if
they had never fallen before.
They might step through mirrors to me
and set all the red leopards running loose
in the temples.... O tricky Lilith,
a jade thrown into the center
of pooled holy water, the disappearance ringed
by widening dreams, marriages to absence
as I roll graved stones away
from gaping eyes and step out in all
my names and disguises, a million,
reviving a vow:
        to make Adam remember how
to ask if eclipse can shine in hiding,
to ask if elapse can come back with pearl's
concentrics, to ask if the serpent
curled at his hearth might earn her warmth
and a proper blessing, to ask
if the waters that wash my heart can be
divided with prayer, walked through, turned red

with defeat, to ask if dream
would barter its wonder for a blood algebra,
if the willow would barter her journal
of excursions through all the zeros
below zero for the moon's arithmetic...
For I would barter my magic
chrysalis for a planter's hands,
my desert panache for a bridal veil,
my blatherings for the cabala's shackles...
O I would barter anything—my whole
bizarre bazaar
                    to make Adam remember
that my life too went on in exile
weaving green sorrows from shapeless abandon
slithering through destructive twilights
and through the mad heats of the Nile,
that I was exiled without company
save what I could make of myself from air.
And I would have Adam consider this:
Solomon bothered to learn my tongue.
I made him laugh; he made me
dance to his laughter
and in the end he joined the dance.
Should one forgetting come out from under
the marriage canopy let him remember
how I bring the spice to espousals,
fierce glitter to the ring,
how I bring bright conclusions to dull
premises, how I bring the eternal triangles
to a point, how I dissolve at the point
of panic,
at the point of loss like the pain
of a joke,
how I transform by lay and by lie the myth
                    that Adam forgets.
What then? Could he make of me
more than an immaculate misconception?
Admit me to his children?
For I would have him let me bear
some reality.

IX. Getting Out / Of The Women / The Children: Lilith finds that her continued relationship with men is not enough to give her the reality of human children, that the only way to fully satisfy her desire and curiosity is to approach the women and children themselves. She tries several methods: she hides in the beds of lovers and scrapes up the spilled sperm to see what she can make out of that; she learns to pose as a midwife and tries to steal the children at birth; she comes to the children, as she has come earlier to the men, at night, teaching them laughter and sexual play. All of this gets her not much more than a bad reputation, yet the charms and oaths invented by the women against her do not vanquish her. In the end she does win the spirits of some of the children to call her own and her spirits (popularly known as Lilis) cry IMI (a Hebrew cry for mother) to her. Lilith has learned through zany persistence to live with herself as a being apart, as she continues to make humanity dream — perhaps more openly — of her crazy freedoms.

IX. *Getting Out / Of The Women / The Children*

(1)

Feeling broody and cross,
I had to use my wit:
the will and the wisp my mediums,
the wither and the weather, changeability, loss,
my crammed adaptitude, the light touch.

So I hid between the marriage sheets,
scraped up the gummy love-spills
by dribs and drabs with my fingernails.
Making do, making do...
and those leftovers, let me tell you,
made indifferent devils,
tattletale offspring disengaging themselves
from me to join my mixed multitudes —
pests, tempters, mad immortals.

Then I stole into birthrooms
disguised and stole so
candidly the women caught on.
They wrote on the walls,

wore charms and scratched in porridge bowls
words against me.
They called up the angels
Senoy, Semangelof, and Sansenoy—
words against me:
"Adam and Eve. Out Lilith."
And I admired their pith,
point blank, and chose to stay.

Of course they never guessed
my one true taming name,
and I managed to bribe the angels
well enough.
I can live with shame.
I can even turn it into love.

(2)

I simply wanted a few embryos,
some usable news of the womb,
some rudiments to make my own.
A *devil may care*.

I offered those mothers what I knew,
but they weren't interested in that
sort of charm. I offered to spin
a room of straw to gold.
I offered to babysit.
What could I do?

I made midnight the nursery hour,
put on my nanny mask and while the moon
played with light fingers on the tiny cots
I tickled and taught the little faces how to smile.
I showed the little fingers where to play.
I taught them how to dream so that someday...

Lilis let there be.
My spirits are on the rise again, this time singing
IMI IMI IMI IMI

O blooming Lilith of the darkest touch
shall be once more wild Lilith
with the wild rose red wild hair,
a devil-may-care.

X. The Odds and Ends of Passion: According to the Zohar, the exiled
Lilith is the "nakedness of the Shekinah," the Shekinah being the feminine
and indwelling spirit of God. Legend develops the figure of "Lilith the
Younger," no longer a figure of the devil but an embodiment of the
Shekinah who is allowed to enter the temple and to inform its sacred space.
Lilith, reinstated finally in this way, looks back over the passion of her
life. There is still some self-pity, regret, and indignation in her, but at last
a certain calm and self-satisfaction for having endured.

x. *The Odds and Ends of Passion*

Even when the trees began to walk
through me, beating
my mirage of hearts
inventing the first rhythms of weeping
and later laughter,
I was meant to be
unwritten, erased, effaced,
the Shekinah in her nakedness.

Nevertheless, I was
the first and more
lithe love, first demeaned,
a white haunch hiding in willow,
a lost wing and riddle in the desert,
a lion-tamer and wild for prophets' tongues,
a lady who made a name for herself,
or thirty dirty names, a lady who,
so suppressed and so mixed in her multitudes,
got even by being odd;
and little credit to God.

After all how can I forget
how I was meant to be
left out,
haphazard whore, bejeweled
scapegoat;
how they called me callous incubus,
failed succubus of Adam,
fit consort for Cain;
how they missed me and misunderstood
how I was meant to be:
the sun dropping its red
last radiance
to the willow bled
into my silence.

Passed around all my lives
like an anti-eucharist;
passed over as an orphan or a widow,
passed under like a secret at high tables,
but never passed away
I finally re-enter my temple,
put on my proper veil.
I am a kind of virgin, the one who
managed with no
manseed to grow
to the shape of a funerary urn:
Lilith the Younger,
making new.

XI & XII. Proposals and *Recreation:* Still the spirit of Lilith, neither
Younger nor Older, cannot be stopped in one place for so long. She goes
on in her imagination to propose her own sainthood beyond the Hebrew
legends already accumulated. She considers that, after all, her passionate
troubles may qualify her as a Saint; she imagines that parts of her body —
even bogus parts — might be turned into relics that would effect miracles.
At the end of her daydream she proposes again to God: that He admit her
creation as valid, that He marry her. This is her first hope and her last,
and all that Adam can do at this point is to look on in puzzled awe and to
end the poem.

XI. *Proposals*

I propose the sainthood of exclusion,
St. Lilith left out to melt in the rain
like the laughter of children as they run.
And I propose the sainthood of accidental creation,
St. Lilith Misshapen of the breathtaking charm;
St. Lilith Cock-a-hoop, born before the Word;
St. Lilith in a million filigreed cradles—
here a fingernail paring, there a pubic hair,
a little shred of the transplanted heart,
a crumb of the hard-won skeleton.

Most precious would be a bit of the rib
sprouted spontaneously, or a single drop
of the spectacular menstrual blood.
The most suspect shred of a life, after all,
has been known to provoke
the wanted miracle.

St. Lilith—sell me door to door, save
your pennies and light me a green candle,
let me into the whispers of the nave,
set me like a ruby in a monstrance—
I should like to hold the Host.

Now for the last time, old bald God,
though a life as crooked as mine
can never be quite straightened out,
I propose to you:
marry me, breathe me in again.

I'll make you an honest man.

XII. *Recreation*

And when Adam saw the sea by night
he sighed...

THE DEPARTURES AND VOICES OF SARAH

for Sarah Hadas

Abraham I can't understand, in a certain sense there is nothing I can learn from him but astonishment.

Kierkegaard, Fear and Trembling

...in all that Sarah hath said unto thee, hearken unto her voice.

Genesis 21:12

And because Abraham and Sarah kept afar from the serpent, Sarah obtained life eternal for herself, her husband and all her descendants after her.... For Sarah attached herself throughout to life, and thus life was made her own.

Zohar, 2

Who can find a virtuous woman? for her price is far above rubies.
    The heart of her husband doth safely trust in her, so that he shall have no need of spoil.
    She will do him good and not evil all the days of her life....
    Strength and honor are her clothing; and she shall rejoice in time to come.
    She openeth her mouth with wisdom; and in her tongue is the law of kindness.
    She looketh well to the ways of her household, and eateth not the bread of idleness.
    Her children arise up, and call her blessed; her husband also, and he praiseth her.
    Many daughters have done virtuously, but thou excellest them all.
    Favor is deceitful, and beauty is vain: but a woman that feareth the Lord, she shall be praised.
    Give her of the fruit of her hands; and let her own works praise her in the gates.

Proverbs 31:10–12, 25–31

The First Departure: marrying Abram

I knew before I married him
he wasn't such a good catch as my mother said.
I'd seen him—my uncle—in the marketplace
hawking wooden figures of Nimrod's gods.
I saw him laugh in an old woman's face
because she wanted to buy something holy. Sad.
Idols. It was a respected old family business,
though not such a fine one as my mother said.
Toy gods never suited Abram.

Anyway, I did marry him.
He is terribly far-sighted, while I am near,
which means he never gets a very good look at me.
He fell in love with my mind and sense of humor,
so he says, and never even asked about my dowry.
No head for figures, and he likes to play with fire.
Yet I love him for his honest absurdity;
near-sighted as I am, I can see him going far.
There's somemhing like a wizard in Abram.

It was just after I married him
King Nimrod, offended at Abram's attitude, sent word
to his father Terah employed at court, to bring him there.
Terah agreed—don't ask me why—so Abram came forward
and said his god could quench even Nimrod's fire.
Ox-headed Abram. I was very scared.
They threw him in a furnace. But Abram walked on air,
the flames blooming up to a garden. He had the last word,
and I am very proud of Abram.

I am glad I married him,
against all common sense and even now,
when life in Ur has gotten so dangerous for us.
Abram's Holy One says, "Get thee out," and so we go.

In Nimrod's furnace my own father turned to ash.
But we take Terah, my brother Lot, a small retinue
of slaves and animals, what we can of the house.
It's hard to leave, against all sense, but then as now,
I put my hand in Abram's.

ב
Landed and Dispossessed: giving the bride away

Shechem, Moreh, Bethel, Ai, Hebron, Moriah, on and on.... The rou-
tine: haShem's altar first, my tent, then his, then Lot's; local bargains,
small cattle pastured; please haShem, let this stay be long. It never is.
Welcome wears and I begin to learn arrival and possession are frames of
mind; leavetaking is half of greeting. Skin olive-oiled, and still I dry out
like Hebron's fields, cracked with time and sunburn, spread out under
Abram like a map, trampled by whim, barren as if, color sucked out by
sun and moon, nothing in relief. So well-travelled, I feel my self stretch
thinner with each thin land we leave. Abram tells me the last famine is ha-
Shem's sign. I obediently swallow all he says. It becomes me.

For Abram there is nothing that is not a sign. Pushed to extremes by
these we cross the Nile's seven arms dragging a dream of Abram's: trees
and men with hatchets. Abram is afraid. He is the cedar. I am the palm.
It is too complicated to explain. I weep all night before the entry. At
dawn as I wash smeared dust away at the water's edge I hear a gasp and
turn to see Abram behind me staring in the stream where my face lies
shattered by splash. It's as if he'd seen Pharaoh with sword upraised. His
eyes meet mine from his distance, brief as falling stars, and drop to his
feet. "You are beautiful," he shrieks, "put on your veil or they will kill me
to have you, the meaning of the dream. Say you are my sister. No, a better idea. That trunk. I'll hide you—here—get in—you're cargo, personal
effects—I don't know why I never saw..."

Egypt, I have heard, is like Eden. It is not until this reflection—I now see
he sees—that even Abram can fall into the forbidden feeling. I am not to
see or be seen. In the dark my stomach turns, my heart's uneven as the

seeming spastic limps of the men that heave the casket, my head swivels
back and forth like a telltale to their sync-less beat. At last — they thud me
down at the customs gate.

"What's in here?" A rapping pierces me. "Barley," says my husband far
away. "We think it's more than that." I feel their winks. Abram offers to
pay the tax on wheat. On silk. On pepper. What am I worth my weight
in? On gold. I smile to myself. Finally — I can hear the strain in his throat
— on rubies, if they will not look. But then they force the lock. It is as if I
am reborn, the relief after the sickening dark. It's that, I'm sure, made
them later tell Pharaoh how I shone. "She is my sister," said my husband,
giving me away. I did not give him away.

ל
Seeing Through: an exodus

I made Pharaoh send my "brother" pearls and sheep,
slaves, oxen, precious metals, all those commodities
that, unlike me, are not too good to keep.

I was supposed to marry Pharaoh, but he got sick.
I humor him and pretend to read his fevered dreams.
Through this I see: his plague is more than bad luck.

One night he dreams a princess trailing a cloud
across a desert. He follows. A hermit creeps after him.
He feels the evil eye and the woman draws a sword.

As Pharaoh nears, she reaches up and slits the soft gray
belly of the cloud. Something breaks like an egg on his head.
Thick blood smothers him. "The fish is amiss in a mummy

land and death's in my hand like a fish-hook," the hermit
laughs. "Judgment lies at the hairline," says the princess.
Pharaoh feels himself dissolve and wakes in a sweat.

The time was right. "Do you give up?" I tease, "It's easy:
I am the princess, and the hermit—remember my brother Abram?—
the shrinking one, who took your gifts and skulked away

with too many thanks? He gave up a wife for dear life. I am she.
His god hides in the cloud and will do you in if I don't
go back to Abram, save him from a hermit's fate. You see,

he was lax of the leisure to look at me. Until—
don't ask why—we crossed the Nile. My looks struck him
like catastrophe, acute possession, to be taken, as evil...

But he does have a direct line to the cure-all. Should he pray
for you, the plague that makes you limp will be lifted
from you along with me. And you will regret it if we stay."

So Pharaoh gives, in exchange for prayer, cold escort to the border.
Shocked and angry as he is (and has a right to be), he is impressed
by invisible power. His last gift to me is his daughter Hagar.

Abram sees Pharaoh punished for his wistful tantamount crime.
I feel the household punished for my presence and my pose.
Egypt was all a dream. But whose? Abram's or mine?

ד

Entrances and Exits: our separate ways

i

On the other side of the Nile we wake each other up,
get used to each other again, pick up our broken promises
and stick them back together. I learn to do without
doves' tongue dishes, silk soft as moth-fur, gazelles
in my private garden, Pharaoh's songbirds and musicians.
But Abram living alone had gotten plenty of habits
and hobbies he couldn't drop: astrology, magic, fooling around
with the alphabet and the mother tongue. Scribe, script
and scroll, he mumbos his jumbo and scratches in the clay
I smooth for him: circles, walls, and bodies with all

entrances and exits marked, matched columns of days and gates
of the face, light and dark, right and left, man and woman.
He scribbles little crowns on everything, talks in tokens:
Merit, Fire, Law, Mothers, Guilt and Crypt and Water...

Where does he get such ideas?

ii

I, too, hold the cosmos by a hand put in my hand,
speak with all the voices that I can and ride the universe
like a camel until blood drains from my ceaseless sway
and the undulations of the weather, month after moony maze.
Arrival and departure.

There are patterns in my mind, too. Air, skeleton; water, muse;
fire, riddle; the wind, the water jar, and the bone left over
are mine in the name if Iscah—my pet of names given me
by my father, as I stare so hard—at starlight, diversity, flower...
I find the gates of Binah.

Gates of compassion and mother wit manifest in and under
the Shekinah's wings where mysteries of faith are mysteries
of sex, as a wifeless prophet is haShem apart from *Yod* and *He*.
The riddle is divide to multiply. What first, letters or lays?
I ask the Shekinah.

ה

Another Seeing Through: choosing different lots

Abram believes in the only one.
He wants to be the only one.
I would be many if not barren.

    I've loved being near my brother Lot
    while Abram is off surveying his promise.
    The two of us sing songs we learned in Ur
    as children, tell jokes, take walks, sip tea.

When Abram's around we learn to keep quiet.
He's been so touchy about the three of us
being too close, yet Lot's his only heir.
The flocks increase and multiply; not I.

There's plenty in this promised land, but just
for one. Lot's herdsmen and Abram's squabble
like serpent and soul. There's jealousy everywhere,
set off by generosity. Abram suggests
separation; Lot agrees to set off for fertile
Jordan. I lift up my eyes. And nothing there.

Abram is the chosen one,
the choosy one, the lonely one.
I have not chosen to be alone.

ר
A Gift for War: the thrift of love

What kind of wife would be eager for her husband to go to war?
Who understands the politics? who Amraphel and Arriwuku,
Chadorlaomer, Beara of Sodom, or Birsha of Gomorrah are?
Word from Sodom to the oaks of Mamre: Lot's in trouble there.
So, Abram must go to the rescue—it's his only nephew.
To worry—it's only natural.
                              So you sit and you wait for news.
They say the planet Zedek made a fog of weird light
all around Abram as he fought. Can you believe what you hear?
And that Layla—some kind of angel—let him see right
through her, and the swords of his enemies dissolved in air
like salt in water. You could see even their arrows evaporate.
But when Abram throws just a handful of sand, every grain
turns into a javelin!
                      Ah, but half of the things I hear
I don't believe. So they make up stories to keep up their spirit.
This I understand. I wonder—where was this magic in Egypt? War!
Who needs it?

And then, a woman likes to see a memento, a souvenir.
But listen—after all those nice victories, what does Abram do?
Bring home an expensive knicknack, as much as a candlestick? No.
Yet the King of Sodom himself, they say, said, "Take everything."
Only Abram has with haShem some kind of promise, not to.

One thing
I've learned from experience: never to pass up or to throw away
so much as a sandal thong or piece of camel's hair, worn linen,
used nails, apple cores, ashes...so there must have been
something he could have picked up—half a cloak-buckle maybe,
a silk tassel...

Now the last thing Abram needs, I know,
is a complaining wife; yet how can he come home all holier-than-thou
empty-handed? and not even thinking how I must have suffered?
Men do not often appreciate...

Still, I am very glad
he did not fall into a slime pit.

And then Melchizedek, a nice man and wealthy, a king,
took a liking to Abram, taught him libations and burnt offerings,
all sorts of tricks. Later, maybe remembering how Abram
took nothing from Sodom, he sends along the little fur suits
Adam and Eve wore, saved by Noah's wife, the mother of Shem
(from whom I myself descend), who knew how to invest
in the future and how her children's children might have a use
for these hand-me-downs. In the old days things were made to last.
So—something can come from war I guess.

I accept...what is fair.

ר

Bits and Pieces: a covenant of One and one

Then one day I am looking up the hill from my tent-door
and there is Abram cutting in half his best heifer,
a ram and a nice nanny goat, the way he sometimes does
when other rich men come to settle some business.
You'd think he would mention it to me. He is all alone.
Naturally vultures come. He jumps up and down like a crazy man.

As the birds fly off he suddenly sags and stretches out
beside the rows of meat. To take a nap? I don't like it.
It could be the sunstroke again. I start to think about
bringing him his hat and maybe some nice lamb broth, but
when I get there...
                         His eyes are glazed open; he will not
blink when I wave my hands like this, or answer. I sit
with his head in my lap. It is quiet as a cave. The smell of blood
makes my head ache. When twilight comes I decide
to fetch Eliezer before wild dogs come to have him carry
Abram to my tent. Halfway there I look back and what do I see?
a sort of torch floats along between the stinking hunks.
I forget Eliezer, go back. Abram is leaning against the trunk
of the olive tree, head tipped, counting, counting. "Sarai,"
he says, "help me count them, the stars, look at how many..."

He has been lying there nearly dead not to mention scaring me
out of my wits and acting like he's had the evil eye on him
and now he calmly asks me to count stars. "Look here, Abram,"
I say (I am not hiding that I am upset), "this is going too far.
Study, study, study. Without enough exercise, without fresh air,
ruining your only pair of eyes. So is it a big surprise
you fall down in a fit? Look at this bloody mess.
Tell me something—are you proud of this?"
                                          "Oh, yes,"
he says, "yes, yes, yes, yes, yes. The Holy One
has come to seal this covenant with me—He came in person—
and He promised me my children and their children and...
They are to be as many as stars or grains of sand."

Infinity! So many. Who needs this? Just one single
star, just one grain of sand—for me that would be enough.
Not for Abram. For years cooped up, thinking too much,
scratching in his codes, listening for the invisible,
studying, studying, looking so hard for a voice...

So when has he had time to be a father?
He expects me to listen with a straight face?
Stars in his eyes, or sand—it's a wonder
he can see anything at all.

ה
One Plus One: union and separation `

Mornings when Abram sings to his Sepher Yetzirah,
  Evenings when my love is in his mind's patterns,
Am I supposed to enjoy talking to myself? I do.*
  Hermit plus serpent are two.

This is the union:
One by myself I make up the feeling of plus.
  Sarai is small cattle princess, tent peg, flax.
  Iscah is the eye of Eve, a sweet tooth, nakedness.
Sarai and Iscah are one with stylus in hand.
  In creation proper no one is alone:
    Elohim, Adam, Adamah are one.
    Adamah, Eve, and Sarai are one.
    Sarai and Iscah and laughter are one.
Iscah's book is made of scatterings all over.
The stories Sarai tells are one-day wonders.

This is the separation:
Abram sways with concentration in his tent;
  Sarai plays with murmurs and stirs them in the soup.
Abram invents what to make of the alphabet;
  Sarai weeps it out of shouts and laughs it inside out.
  Iscah polishes sight with tears and cheers like wind in laurel.
He learns by head what she knows by heart.
So much for him.

* See Appendix I: *fragments from the Book of Iscah.*

ט

Gifts and Gratitude: second thoughts about generosity

i

Talk about sacrifices! I do my best to believe
and do everything according to what haShem says
to Abram that we must do in order to conceive.

All day I am running from here to there—
and I am not as young as I used to be—
to fetch for the altar, to prepare, to prepare.

And then—may my ears fall off if it is not
true—I overhear my darling at his prayers:
"It were better I be childless," he says. *Than what?*

I'd like to know. He goes on, "than that a child
of mine, Lord, should offend thee." Tell me, does he
bother to ask me for my opinion? I work and I build

up my strength and hope to have everything thrown
away by a cringing lick-spittle like that, dismounting
on both sides of the camel: "I'd like to have a son,

but if it's too much trouble...? and if he gives you
an ulcer, Lord, what then? or the earth—would it be
ruined perhaps—with my infinity?" I'm through

with endless flirting with goodness. I hear haShem laugh.
Marriages aren't made in Heaven; it's blood and tears right here.
Children, also. *Here.* I have had enough of *what if.*

If he can't believe with me, let him try with Hagar.

ii

HaShem knows how
        I have suffered to be a good wife to you, Abram,

and with moving every other week.
Who knows why?

I'm not so dumb.
Don't think I can't see the sly looks you give
my maid Hagar—and she's no lambkin either—
I have my pride.

I've tried to keep
your promise in my body, but the way it's falling out
like fallow sand, it's a waste of time. Once near the Nile
you gave me up,

out of keeping
with the youthful expectations I might have had.
So now I offer you Egypt back. Exile yourself in her.
I'm able to bear

the truth at least.
Her child could be mine to raise, born on my knees
by law, where wives run dry and husbands yearn
for second best.

So this is it.
I hope I am not a selfish person. What do I ask
in return? Gratitude? Listen, gratitude—I have had—
and I can do without.

iii

Abram, listen. I thought I was too old
to change. I was wrong. My heart's not gold.
As I said, I didn't expect gratitude.

But I didn't expect to lose my face
to this slave's. Let's just get something straight.
This woman used to wash my feet.

What right has she to hoot and twitter behind my back?
Sway-belly. Warty melon. Who's she to mock?
She's knocked up. So I should be a laughing stock?

"My Lady Sarai can't *conceive* of it,"
she mewls with her mulish spurt of wit,
"but my lord has a taste for forbidden fruit."

So how come your High and Mighty sticks a bun
in *her* oven and not in mine? What has *she* done
I haven't done for you? Fat tick. Hanger-on.

Has she worried herself sick about your eyes?
Has she had to tell fibs and make sacrifices
to protect Your Majesty? What kind of a god is this

who makes one woman to put another down?
Here I am, only ninety. I should have known
it wouldn't work. I can't help the sin

of dropping needles in her bed, throwing shoes
in her face, spilling hot oil accidentally on her thighs,
casting evil eyes. You've heard—screeches like lilies.

You think I enjoy it? Someone's got to go. I can't share.
I hate myself for this. I set her hair on fire.
Sometimes I hear her cry at night, and I don't care.

Abram, you and haShem, you must choose between us two.
I'm past the age when it's fun to be a shrew,
and I'd rather have no child than hers. It won't do.

Abandon her. Hide her at least until
she's delivered the burden that makes me so cruel.
Send her away for the sake of my soul.

I am begging you.

A Very Hard Thing To Understand: a bloody husband

So Hagar left and things calmed down. HaShem called her back. She kept
her place, she shared her son, and that was that. Could I find energy to
care any more? I should live so long. Then one ordinary morning Abram
sticks his head in my tent as usual, but with an extraordinary look in his
eye. "Well, haShem spoke again last night," "Oy—what now," I whisper,
as I have had it up to here with his singular infinities, visions of grandeur,
promises, promises... Abram looks sheepish for a minute—a look I'm
partial to, I admit—then gravely leans the five fingertips of his right hand
against the five of his left, spread like a cone of faggots under a sacrifice,
and drones in his most cryptic voice: "Scribe and script and scroll in my
hands are joined in life as my three and three above and come to their
points; the circle with thumbs is the unsung fundament letter or cipher
incised in flesh like a wedding ring of blood: this is covenant, ark, bow,
breast, the ten ineffable Sephiroth... Shhh, don't tell." And he winks.

Can I help it if this is the way he talks, particularly after a long night studying? He is ninety-nine years old, after all, and entitled... So what am I
expecting? A little bonfire under the tamarisks maybe, with something
special to say over the ram's ashes after. Nothing much. So imagine my
surprise. In the afternoon I am going out to get some water, and there is
Abram standing at his tent-door with some of his cronies all swaying
back and forth as if in wordless prayer or toothache, biting coarse camel
blankets or sandal leather, some cupping hands between their thighs.

Abram is spotted all over with blood, hands caked purple-brown, robe
tucked at his waist and blood trickling down one leg. "Sarai..." he begins,
thinking maybe I don't see him hiding the knife behind his back. "Sarai,
this is just..." The rest is mumbled, but I see. "You have cut your *what?*"
I shriek. "Sarai... just a little piece, a little skin... haShem said..." "Ha-
Shem couldn't be satisfied with your body the way He made it? It wasn't
doing something it was supposed to be doing? It isn't enough you offer to
go childless for His Name's sake, counting stars like an idiot? May the
Shekinah sharpen her wings on your back, and do like this to your neck!"

How was I to know it would be all right? Nothing
haShem told him to do ever brought me any closer

to motherhood; nothing had ever brought him so close
to womanhood, barren and cowed and dripping...
He is in pain. I bring him to my tent and light
the lamp and hold him close. We are in the same boat.
So, so. Bloody husband and barren wife, past bearing
the hurt alone.

Let me just say that this is a very hard thing
for me to understand.

ב

Mutter and Babble: back and forth to children

"Aleph, Mem, Shin:
      Ox, Water, Tooth;
            mothers with the tongue the two:
Merit and Guilt: Truth
      shuttles between the three of them:
            mutes, sibilants, others..."

Abram is still muttering to himself this way.
Maybe to ease the pain. Yesterday haShem
spoke to him by name—He opened *Abram*
with a *ha*! and showed him to smooth *Sarai*
to *Sarah*. Then Abraham seemed fresh as the day
he strolled in Nimrod's fire-garden,
his life before him and before him
I feel a new space within.

It makes us laugh to see each other
so new—once more we spend the night
holding hands, our palms pressed tight
as children do—giggling over nothing.
He had to come to Hagar under cover
I joke, but now he will be coming
to me uncloaked, smooth-skinned as a
boy, not yet grandfather.

ל

A Stranger Mystery: sustaining hospitality

And I have to laugh the next day too, as long as I see
Abraham humming to himself, content in the dog-day sun
at his tent-door. But then he leaps up and shades his eyes
toward the distance. I know what he wants—not that I do—
and my smile fades as the strangers—three—come into view.
Nothing goads Abraham out of self-pity like someone to entertain.
He gestures madly, scampers out to meet them, leads them back
and makes them comfortable under one of the oaks. I know
what's coming next: "Sarah—three good measures—for cakes—
and hurry—they can't stay all night."

> A stranger is a Mystery,
Abraham likes to say, and so is his hospitality, to me.
But we must partake. We are here to serve. So be it, though
I wonder—does he have to kill three perfect calves just so
these transients dressed like Arabs can each one have
a tongue with mustard? Must he roast an ox? For the love
of haShem! He should treat his own household half so well.

I don't want to complain, but to be honest, I don't feel
so well today. Far be it from me, however, to spoil a party.
So here I am, mixing the batter, setting it aside, shaking
sour whey in a skin. And there is ridiculous Abraham—scarcely
healed—running, fetching, carrying, worrying, waiting
just like a woman. I bleed for him.

> Meanwhile
I feel like I've eaten too many unripe figs
or been kicked in the stomach. I feel...between my legs...
Oh. It is more than a metaphor—I actually bleed for him—
But the ember-cakes in the oven! I have tainted them!
How strange. It's been decades since I've stained a thing.
I cannot serve them now—but then Abraham will wonder—
and if I tell—he will be adamant—about such a matter—
and what will *they* make of me?

> I hear them laughing.

Mother and Other: seeing through laughter

I tag behind the servants who carry the plates
of dainties — excluding the ember-cakes of course —
then wait out of sight by the tent-flap to listen.
Would it be terrible to interrupt the conversation?
I do not usually eavesdrop, but in an emergency...
One of the strangers is predicting Abraham's son,
my son, and in a year from now. Sure thing. I am ninety.
Abraham...? is ninety-nine.
>   Ha!
>   I laugh.
>   I laugh behind the tent-flap —
>   to myself, I hope —
>   could they hear it?
I rush then into the quiet-as-death quiet
all at once eager to fill it up.

"We were about to ask after you, Sarah," states
one unintroduced as names are being mumbled by Abraham.
I look at their plates.
They are eating like birds, all of them.
And the one — called Michael, I think it is —
not enough even to fill
a goldfinch. I am afraid I seem nervous.
I suggest a smidgen of this or that — or are they full
already — maybe room for just some sesame
butter, grapes, dates... a sliver of melon? some honey?
Are the words coming out or not?
They are not eating enough even to make
decent scarecrows out of them. But all right. All right.
Maybe they were too busy talking. Maybe they are not
used to the food. Gabriel, just a little more?
I am not asking if they want any cake.
The silence — an enormous belly.
>   "What I came for" —
I turn to my husband — "is to say I'm sorry,
but the cakes are not fit for you to eat.

By that I mean"—I turn to the guests—"my husband is
allergic—not quite—but if you have no objection
to something made up by a woman in question,
I can wrap some up for you to take for later?"
"By all means, and thank you very much," says
the one called Michael. "But now have a cup of wine with us."
Abraham coughs. I blush.
                              And Raphael says, "Sarah, why
did you laugh just now?" "Laugh," I say,
"who laughed? The wind in that tree...? Maybe Lilith..."
"But you *did* laugh," says Gabriel staring through me.
Michael looks at his plate and looks devious.
"All right, I heard you joking about us.
We are ninety and ninety-nine years old, after all,
old enough to beware of prophets that are false.
Is it a nice thing to do, to tease
an old man, and when he is being so generous?"

"You laughed."

"So? So I laughed. I admit it. I am the daughter
of a man, and the wife, but—now—to be the mother
of a multitude—it breaks me up—that's life."

I feel like a grenadilla bud about to burst.

"And I laughed because I already knew,
by a certain untimely curse that..." and I blush
again to think of the untouchable cakes.
Abraham chokes.
                    His strange guests get up to go.
I bleed for him.
                  It is too much, too much...
*So I laugh.**

* See Appendix II: *another reason.*

Emergency and Well-wishing: for the sake of argument

I watch alone as Abraham sees them out to the oak
that marks our pasture's far edge. They hesitate
to shuffle last words as guests do at thresholds extending
superfluous thanks, weather forecasts, and well-wishing.

Then two—Gabriel and Raphael I seem to make out—head
toward Sodom and the one called Michael stays on to talk.
He and Abraham have gotten off the good-bye see-saw
apparently. They begin to stiffen and then throw

their arms about, locking in poses like prophets.
I've too much to think about already. I want my husband
alone with me, right now. But he's so lost in thought
by the time he wanders back it's hard to draw out

what was so drawn out out there. Finally he explains:
as Gabriel and Raphael were about to set off for Sodom
Michael became unquiet, brought up the evils of the city,
the perverted lack of hospitality, the way any charity

is punished there by death—even I have heard the story
of the girl who smuggled bread to an old beggar
by the well and how they dipped her in honey and stuck her
on the wall to be swarmed to death by bees and laughter

was her only epitaph. Abraham says he got the feeling
while Michael was raging on that he heard haShem's voice
(as well he might—he's heard it so often lately)
planning Sodom's total destruction and his mind naturally

goes to our poor Lot and his family there and for once
Abraham has to stand up to haShem. He insists what if
there happen to be fifty good souls in a doomed place,
must they die like the rest, whimsically, be a sacrifice

for them? He sees haShem considering. No. So Abraham,
for the sake of argument, bargains him down: forty-five?

thirty? twenty? ten? HaShem says he would save it
for ten. Abraham feels he's won. They leave it at that.

So what is so terrible? It is all only theoretical,
isn't it? But just in case, I make Abraham send Eliezer
after the two—whoever they really are—to investigate.
The news of our child... I had wanted to celebrate,

but now it's all overshadowed. Abraham is much more
excited about his debate with haShem and abstract punishments
than about any private eventuality. Again I am left out
with my inner emergency. He stands up for humanity, yet...

ט

*Taking In and Throwing Out: a lot of trouble**

What an awful thing. What a hard thing
to understand. Hospitality, now—
hospitality I understand—even if it is a lot of trouble
to take in somebody you maybe don't even know—

so I guess Lot was right to invite the strangers in,
as it is only proper for a person of his background,
even if they happen to frown on this in Sodom.
But why, why, when angry Sodomites surround

his house yelling for him to throw the strangers out...
He might have asked his guests if they would mind
explaining themselves to the mob. Did he even offer
to introduce them? No. He out-philistined

the Philistines—don't ask me why—and offered
instead—of all things—to sacrifice his only two
daughters, virgins, to that rabble scrambling to ram
down his door. Now. I ask you,

* See Appendix III: *speculations.*

what if these strange guests had not had the power
of haShem to strike the wild men blind?
Lot could have lived with this?
What about Idith? Were they both out of their minds?

Then Lot was ordered to scram with his family
while the mob still rubbed their eyes—before the final doom
that same night—and not to look back—just go, hurry up—
but Idith, poor soul, did turn to mourn her home

such as it wasn't, under flames and clouds of sulfur,
and she hardened to a ramrod of tears no promise could melt.
So Lot left her there for small cattle to lick and men
to make jokes about. What was she worth? Salt?

Wanting to take it with you, wanting to be abandoned,
to save, to give up... I know just how she felt.
Why go on? It's too hard a thing to understand.
Can spectacles do anything but harden? Was it her fault

she wanted to see? A temptation so real I can taste it.

ע

In Light of Extinction: from Sodom to Gerar

Since the nastiness over Sodom our road
is not much traveled. Oh, sometimes a shepherd
does happen by, but the talk is never good—
just rumors—Sodom, Lot's daughters—we've had

enough. The garden's gone, blown full of ash
from Sodom. Either that is poison, or
Hagar has cast her evil eye—that shameless
briberess of false prophets, seed-corn parcher.

Over the years you learn some things: how best
nod when he announces the move, and sigh

when he straps the star-charts on his back,
packs the alphabet stones you'd hoped he'd lost,
and ask: "In all your caskets of oracles, why
is there no room for the book *I'd* like to take?"

You learn to ask, as if you've any interest,
"Will the new place have a respectable market?
As good as Beer-sheba maybe? Or adequate?"
You learn to be dressed against sunstroke, dressed

against sunburn; you learn how to limp on
both feet when he asks you to walk, but still there is
something you are never prepared for—this
is that you must lie, "I'm his sister"—his skin

being at stake, and olive oil will not keep him
from losing it. This is the part of exile
I hate. It makes me available to any king
and, to be frank, my heart goes out to Abimelech. He should be punished for thinking
I'm beautiful? I hate all this—denial.

I say, "Never again!" Then it happens again.
Is it nice I should be the source of pestilence?
For my sake haShem makes this kingdom barren.
This much I appreciate—that impotence

is God-given. I think my husband is—
Lord forgive me—smug, and rather pleased
that note of my beauty should result in this.
His imagination, maybe, is diseased?

How many times does he have to pull it off?—
giving me up 'til they're begging him, take her back
(along with cattle, silver even, slaves and more)
when they see that having me is making them sick.
It makes *me* sick. As we're riding out of Gerar,
smoke rises yet in the distance, puff after fatal puff.

"And Sarah said, 'God has made laughter for me; everyone who hears will laugh over me.'"   Genesis 21:6

Back under Mamre's homey oaks,
one month to go, and I'm just a barrel
of laughs.
Almost delivered, and still
I tremble—the original joke's
on us.

More laughter to come, more trembling—
at my age, not to take anything
for granted—
and by a labor of laughter I managed
to push the perfect head
between my blue-veined thighs
that once all Egypt wanted
to praise.

Screams of laughter from all
sides save me from screaming alone
as the body slips out whole
and incomprehensibly begotten
as a perfect quip
with its long long story behind it
like an afterbirth
on every body's lips
as the pale alphabet etched
indelibly on the still stretched
papyrus of my belly invents
the birthcry.

The miracle: I am
a multitude—ha!—in my emptiness,
like Lady Asherah of the Sea,
wetnurse to princes and prophetess,
her thighs astride her donkey
under a laughing laurel tree.

The midwife snuggles a bundle
into my arms; it doesn't giggle,
its eyes shut in the subtle
and perfect mirth of Adam's sleep.
I murmur thanks to the angel
of embryos for this small replica
of Abraham to keep
at my breast opening its abracadabra
mouth where I enter in and lay me down
in a dark warm wordless scroll
and let myself be fed upon
all alone,
multitudes in the tiny syllable
of sucking in.

I have thought and thought about him
in the third person invisible
to myself and to Abraham
and now I am
learning a new use of *you*
of *incomprehensible*
of life and everything utterly new
from haShem.

א

Proof and Plenty: an ingenious entertainment

The cachinnation pales, paroxysm fades
to pang, the mountain of me subsides,
and Abraham, bored by confinement, decides
to throw a party. Every viceroy and king in all
Palestine is invited, with wives and infants, to a ritual
Abraham says will be the final seal
on his fatherhood—no one will call him a sterile mule
the way King Og once did. Already little Isaac's
a spitting image of Abraham, except for one artificial
detail—and this is what he plans to fix.

Eight days old, Isaac lies in the center
of a circle of gifts and guests' wonder.
As Abraham approaches his child a shocked murmur
goes through the crowd at the sight
of the knife (heathen though some still are,
sacrifice of the firstborn is not so fashionable
as it used to be)—is it age or fright
that makes the old man tremble?
I know he does not mean to kill, but still...
the huge blade flashes in the sun.
As it comes down between Isaac's kicking feet
I am almost blinded to the sight
of blood, a tiny spurt like wine jumping out
of a cup set too quickly down.
And that's it.

There is an audible contraction of throats,
as if in reply to a tasteless joke,
and there is that wail that makes my milk
boil down to my nipples' twinge as the opaque
tears begin to seep from those
two blind heavy eyes.

And then the general feast,
but first—inspired by having proved his fatherhood,
Abraham insists I nurse the multitude
of infant guests to prove my motherhood.
I am embarrassed naturally, but nevertheless
I bare my breasts—gigantic loaves, bulking fish—
and barely up from the seabed of childbed
so well-endowed
I satisfy the whole crowd.

Abraham demands credit, as usual,
for himself and the Holy One, the ever-jovial
host of hosts, the genial killer
of fatted calves. I am too tired to care.
As I sneak away from the ovations, Abraham
is having the time of his life. More power to him.
I have never felt so responsible,
so drained of power.

Entertainment and Separation: the method of choosing one

Did I complain to you, Mr. Entertainer-of-the-Century,
when you made that circumcision feast and ordered me
to nurse a league of baby princes? Hostess with the Mostest,
I guess I proved the miracle? But now—weaning—a milkless
feast—in honor, but—and what's your hurry?

Am I supposed to turn off the faucets of the Incredible
Cow?—just like that?—three short years later and still
full to the brim? So who is going to eat up my need
to feed? Dried up, I'll be—sour nut—and I'm afraid
I'll show my age—thin skin even now liable

to spurt at a touch—taut—pod filled like a blister—
then it's all over—and the pain—not in the skin but under—
the slow burn—the ache—when Ishmael offers Isaac
a fresh cool fig—as if he cares—a drink—this is no joke—
and I am just furious with sympathetic Hagar

pretending, and with her pretending son. I'm about to burst—
and there's the pride—there is my son I nursed
taken away and this other—I hurt—can I have Isaac, I ask you,
brought up around such people? Ishmael plays peekaboo
with Isaac even now—laughing—Isaac, the first

and only—in haShem's view and mine—under blood covenant.
So listen, Mr. Give-and-Take-Away, Mr. Love-Everybody-Important,
the plenty in the desert is only there for one... Abraham?
Milk of human kindness dilutes the blood. Since when did haShem
give a damn for equal apportionment?

They must go—agreed? Agreed. This milk—the pressure—empty me.
Wipe your eyes. Remember the guests—you want they should see
you—proud father—like this, milksop—grieving over nothing,
a concubine—a little choice—you'll get over—I am smiling
even with these two hang-dogs—we can't all be

the chosen one, and you must choose
to be one.

The Difference Between Submission and Giving Up: dressing Isaac

So then—just the three—a very happy family—
Isaac growing up—Abraham getting on—haShem cut out
my tongue if I lie—but He makes a fool out
of anyone he chooses—all right—I accept—but suppose
for a laugh—haShem says to Abraham, "Go jump in
the Dead Sea"—I can see Abraham filling his pockets
with stones already...

That look on his face... So haShem is giving him
ideas again—this time a birthday surprise for Isaac:
he gets to go with his father to learn with Shem and Eber—
services, divine names, etcetera—all right I say
if it's not too far—after all, he's only thirty-seven,
a late-bloomer maybe, but smart—so it's about time he finds
how to be on his own—how difficult—and maybe to appreciate
someone to cook, to mend. But be careful I tell him—especially
women—bring her home first—and don't talk to strangers.

The last night—my son comes in my tent—
we sob together like children—"Don't worry about me—
an old woman—I've had my life—you see here?—
my Sabbath lamp, my ornaments—you find a good wife,
it's all hers—my blessing." Isaac hugs me again,
but I'm not fooled. I drag out the battered trunk,
the same I bumped across into Egypt in, hiding my light—
get out the robe Abimelech gave me in Gerar—
the one I wore to hide my big belly that year—
and I dress Isaac in it.

Just like a king he looks—only a little uncomfortable,
as anybody would with such a long journey—and I get out the cloth
I laid the table with for the three strangers—
that time I laughed, and I laugh again
to think—and I wrap it around Isaac's perfect head

against the sun, fasten it with the precious stone
Melchizedek gave to me—from Noah's wife.

So then in the morning—a little picnic basket—
meat and mustard, dates and my special ember-cakes—
the basket I'd carried out of Ur, a little frayed—a bride
I was—with special oils and colored threads and more
charms that never worked for me.

We all stand in the roadway and cry—
"Have a good time," I say—"I don't mind staying home
all alone"—and to Abraham, "Don't let him carry
so much—he is loaded down like a mule already
with the firewood, and be sure and stop to rest—
and in shade—and eat—I will not have any son of mine
come home like a ghost of a ghost or with eyes like holes
burned in a blanket." We kiss again.

I wave and wave. I see them out of sight.
I see them up to no good.
A mother can only do so much

about the uses to which things are put—
the uses—so many—a multitude
I lay my life down in—

and as for the comprehension—
ach, what is that?—to conclude:
to understand a thing—a very hard thing
is what?—to include
whatever may happen—happens—to be at hand
never to waste a thing—
to go on.

ש

Out of Sight in Mind: the delivery at Mount Moriah

So I wave and watch 'til they are small as grains
of sand, and as infinite to my mind.
I have aged more in the last nine hours
than in my ninety barren years.
Meanwhile second sight has grown with this second life.
The price is no more than innocence. It is not right
or wrong I can see, but inevitability.
Abraham sees so far into the distance
all closer things are blurred. HaShem save his eyes.
                              HaShem help his eyes.

My own eyes seem caught in the magic web
of Isaac's robe. After all, I lived in it
in the largest months of my life, and through
the robe I feel his movements now as I did then.
He moves to be finally free of me, step by step
beside his father's self-absorbing prayers.
My husband is determined to deliver a child
to haShem the only way he can, by giving up
some life that belongs to him. He does not understand.
                              He will not understand.

A woman does not understand any better
what makes life come from her and why she must
let go of it. But by labor and sacrifice
of a perfectly natural sort, she gives her gift without
losing sight of it. "Are you sure you want to
let him go?" Abraham said, wanting me to scream "NO"
and so free him from whatever promise. But it's not for me
to hold back consequences. "As I live,"
I said, and I meant it, "try me." And so he does.
                              And thus he does.

As if my third eye were the jewel I fastened
so carefully on Isaac's turban, I see Moriah's peak.

The altar stacked where Cain and Abel tried
to nail down haShem's preference, where Adam
and Noah bound their dreams and bargains...
All altars are the same: highest follies charged
with hopes: over and over and over, the same ground...
Sacrifice happens naturally as the leaves fall
from trees, and if not, not. There is no general point.
                              There is no special point.

Shudders go through my body as if I wore
the flowing robe once more. The labor has begun.
How do I know? Some may say disguised Satan came
to tattle, as if he were a friend of mine!
Some may imagine an angel midwife-detective told.
But a woman knows: she *knows*. Her body is on the line.
The thought of Abraham binding me down to his promise
still strikes strange fire in my head and lets me see
over his busy shoulder. There must be another way.
                              There must be some other way.

It's something Abraham taught me long ago,
whether he knew it or not: that *haShem believes
in metaphor*. Behind the father and son bound by fear
I can see the dumb ram speaking of struggling by being
and its reflection. In some way all things being
equal at the moment of death, the father turns
as if to an annunciation and, able at last to hear;
his thought swells where his son begins to breathe
in relief, once more. The cord is cut. His eyes have cleared.
                              My eyes can shut.

ת

The Space Promise Creates Around Those That It Isolates: *final departure*

Old enough to be finally blind, I stumble away
from my much-patched tent. I say I'm going in search
of my unreturned son. I can't trust Abraham
to bring him home. This is just what I say.

"Believe me," I go on, "I would lie in my tomb
with a smile on my face if I could just see my boy
married and with children. It's high time he stopped
fooling around with this Eber and Shem

and obscure unwritten scripts and scrolls no one
can understand. Who is going to see to it if not his mother?"
This is what I say, so my people will let me go. They think
I must know where I'm headed. "A woman

with a mind of her own," they will nod and smile.
Two of the oldest servants come along with me for company.
No extra shawls, no extra oil. Who cares about the sun?
No picnic basket, no handwork, none of the usual.

So you'd think they could guess. Perhaps they do.
"Her time is up," they will say when I'm out of sight.
Let them. It is. I head toward Hebron. It doesn't matter
where I stop. There's a place I'll be brought to

eventually. HaShem will see to it, I trust.
Long ago, when the messengers came to say what made me
laugh, there was an incident—maybe I forgot to mention—
that was just as funny. The ox Abraham wanted dressed

for the special meal broke loose and ran
and Abraham had to chase it across three fields
or more until finally he managed to corner the beast
in a cave belonging to our rich neighbor Ephron.

There was something about that cave, so later
he went back and there, at the far end, he saw Adam and Eve
stretched out with candles at their heads, reeking of Paradise.
We talked it over and I thought he should offer

as much as four hundred shekels if he could have the whole
field with the cave. At last—after all those years, a place
of our own, a place to be buried in, and with family.
I've thought of it so often. It's good for the soul

to look forward. I have never looked behind
to see where I'm headed. That sadness is not worth my salt.
I weep only in laughing, convulsed toward whatever comes
with wonder. My tears do not harden, but carry me off to find

what, exactly, I cannot say.

Cipher Yet Sarai: fragments from the Book of Iscah

first fragment: a shaggy dog

In the dawn Adamah is and Adam comes to her
  ...in the belly and in the star...
  ...she rolls him in hunger and fear...
  ...flecked and dripping she holds him...
  ...close and far...

Thus Adamah brings the original skeleton out of her closet:
  Upon the One's departure she makes free thus:
Adamah delivers Adam from her ah-ah-ha-ha
  She slices off a syllable and lets him bleed

Adamah the dome is struck by Adam the arrow...

Thus Adamah brings the anxious bones out of Adam's closet:
  ...she puts bugs in his ears and tickles him...
  ...with words he cannot not get...
  ...she cracks her smile like an egg and Adam...
  laughs until his side begins to split...
  ...the bird is hatched: Eve steps out...
  ...to make a long story short...

second fragment: cooking with bay leaves

Adamah is creatrix as Iscah tricks her out;
  As Sarai peers from her tent she hums to herself.

Adamah is building a house out of cedar;
  Sarai makes a space for a child to grow in.

Adamah sits in the belly of the sixth night rejoicing;
  The stars applaud with all their eyes deep dark.

Sarai says a blessing over the light;
    And Iscah opens her eyes in the dark.
Iscah makes a place for wedding words;
    And Sarai fills the Sabbath lamp with oil.

third fragment: the honey moon

Adamah is the honey hive where Adam lolls;
    The never-silent bell presides in Eden's arms.
Praise the Word that comes to double the woman;
    The lamb rejoices to hear the mother's bell.

Adamah is Adam's desire laid bare under a palm tree;
    The father covets the pomegranate with his belly.
Adamah leads Adam to the altar of his manhood;
    Adam watches the evening darken around his lone tree.

Adamah precedes and prepares Iscah's call;
    Her eyes follow free curves of moonlight.
Adamah is the secret name of Eve in her full;
    The Whole One enters by the gate of reflection.

fourth fragment: sealed with a cause

Adamah raises the new man from his bindings;
    The birthcry belongs as much to Abram as Iscah.
Sarai laughs to welcome the seed in her tent;
    Freely the man comes and goes returning joy.

Praise Aleph, Mem, and Shin; water, air, and fire.
    The turtle sings in the scent of the Shekinah's hair.
    The letter rejoices in the sense of the cipher's center.

Adamah is born again and again by syllable;
    Adam rises from each sleep with his hands full,
    The *ah* and *haShem* falling from his tongue.

      Selah

Memo: another reason

And I laughed because there I was,
between my names, between my times,
between my ears, between my eyes,
feeling the hum of my first seclusion
as when my mother's words were glossed
by my body's aching signature.
                                        A man,
she said, would come to my hearth;
a child, she said, would give me birth.
And she told me about a woman's bone.

It was all invisible, save for the blood.
It was all intangible, save for the pain.
It was all inaudible, save for the laughter
as she told me what she would tell my father:

When he asks for you I will say
I have no child by the name of Sarai,
but I have dressed a strange woman today.

And together we laughed between ourselves,
beside ourselves, inside ourselves.
There we were, ready to hold our own,
men coming to their conclusions alone.

first speculation: on creation and destruction

I laughed, but it wasn't so funny really.
I felt my sagging breasts,
one in each boney hand, like a parody
of the Canaanite Astarte, queen of fertility,
and I thought of Abraham, gnarled as the oak roots
his father Terah used to carve
into those fallible idols that fell apart, rotted...
Then someone spoke to me softly as the shiest guest:
"Is haShem too aged to give birth?"
And I began to giggle.
                    Creation, destruction—both
promise and final design—are ridiculous
to those who have no authority...what on earth
is not a miracle?

          "And would haShem really wreck all of Sodom?"
          "He could," says Abraham.
          "But our Lot is there."
          "Don't worry. I've sent Eliezer for news."
          "But the *question* is..."

If a body is sick unto death
except for one single finger,
should the whole body continue to suffer
for the sake of that tiny health?

          What is the difference between
          destruction and sacrifice? Knowing what for?
          Is one and not the other whole?
          What is the difference between promise and perfection?
          Is it time? As Abraham's wife,

perfection has never been all
I wanted to live for.

Is it for the sake of argument or life?
What is the difference?

second speculation: on negative capability

Suppose the stranger we entertain
is straight from haShem or haShem Himself—
does that explain
why Lot would offer to turn his own daughters out
into a battering mob of men
rather than put the perfect stranger out of his house?

> *the stranger inside is a comfort*
> *as women will conceive*
> *the stranger outside is a danger*
> *as men will believe*

Why is it men are so prone
(some men—the ones the Holy One seems to love)
to give up their own
wives and children, hope, dignity, and home,
getting everything ass-backwards,
as far as I can see, from Ur to Egypt to Sodom?

> *for the stranger outside haShem is*
> *as men do believe*
> *the stranger inside I am*
> *trying to conceive*

How can men push life outside
if they never take it in? They try,
but the price paid
is life's whole perspective. A woman is not made blind
by mystery so easily. She takes him by the hand.

third speculation: on a lot of gossip

You thought you'd heard the worst of our Lot?
Not yet. Eliezer heard just the other day
they ended up in Zoar, the two girls and Lot.
Not exactly a friendly neighborhood. So now who
could he find to marry in a place like that?

So now all three are living in a cave, filthy with a lot
of snakes probably, and the rumors are
that he's become no more than a tool in his daughters' plot
to increase and multiply. For them there was no other
man, even after his betrayal of them, even after that.

There was no other man on earth but Lot
who could enter that cave and carry them back
in time to the place where Adam in his single lot,
having no other bride than the one born of his bone,
took her who in turn took him and gave him the fruit

of her wild nature's labor—and hence—our lot.

THE PASSION OF
RAHEL VARNHAGEN

Rahel Levin Varnhagen von Ense (1771–1833)

What a history! — A fugitive from Egypt and Palestine, here I am and find help, love, fostering in you people. With real rapture I think of these origins of mine and this whole nexus of destiny, through which the oldest memories of the human race stand side by side with the latest developments. The greatest distances in time and space are bridged. The thing which all my life seemed to me the greatest shame, which was the misery and misfortune of my life — having been born a Jewess — this I should on no account now wish to have missed.

Words said on her death bed by Rahel
(Antonie Friederike Robert) Varnhagen von Ense,
as reported by her husband Karl August Varnhagen von Ense.

The woman does not actually judge; she has *the subject, and insofar as she does not possess it, it does not concern her.*

Goethe, referring to Rahel's comments on his work —
published excerpts from her correspondence with Varnhagen.

No philanthropic list, no cheers, no condescension, no mixed society, no new hymn book, no bourgeois star, nothing, nothing could ever placate me.... You will say this gloriously, elegiacally, fantastically, incisively, extremely jestingly, always musically, provokingly, often charmingly; you will say it all very soon. But as you do, the text from my old, offended heart will still have to remain yours.

Rahel Levin

1771, May 19	Rahel born in Berlin, eldest child of well-to-do merchant Markus Levin. The family is Orthodox, speaks Yiddish.
c. 1790	Father's death.
1794	Rahel visits relatives in Breslau, is appalled.
c. 1790–1806	Rahel's salon in an attic room on Jägerstrasse to which almost all the important intellectuals of Berlin come: the Humboldt brothers, Friedrich Schlegel, Friedrich Gentz, Schleiermacher, Prince Louis Ferdinand of Prussia and his mistress, Friedrich August Wolf, Jean Paul, Brentano, the Tieck brothers, Chamisso, Fouqué, etc.
1795–96, winter	Rahel meets Count Karl von Finckenstein. Engagement protracted until 1800.
c. 1800	Rahel's brother Ludwig baptized. He assumes the name Robert.
1801	Rahel meets Friedrich Gentz.
1801–02	She meets the secretary of the Spanish Legation, Don Raphael d'Urquijo, and is engaged to him.
1804	Break with Urquijo.
1806, October 27	Napoleon enters Berlin. The war causes Rahel's circle of friends to break up. Soon after the wealth of the Levin family is reduced.
1808, spring	Rahel begins relationship with Karl August Varnhagen.
1809, spring	Rahel meets Alexander von der Marwitz.
1809–11	Varnhagen rises in the military as an accomplished attaché.
1810	Rahel starts calling herself Rahel Robert.
1811	Varnhagen takes Rahel from Berlin to Teplitz.
1814, summer	After travels, publications of correspondence between Rahel and Varnhagen concerning Goethe, more travels due to war, and severe illness, Rahel gets together with Varnhagen again at Teplitz.
1814, September	Rahel returns to Berlin, is baptized, and is married to Varnhagen. She takes the name Antonie Friederike.
1815, September 8	Goethe calls on Rahel in Frankfurt.
1821–32	Berlin salon of the Varnhagens. Prominent visitors: Bettina von Arnim, Heine, Prince Bückler-Muskau, Hegel, Ranke, Eduard Gans.
1833, March 7	Rahel dies.

I. A Present for Schlemihls

« *My history begins earlier than my life, and that is the case with everyone who understands his life.* »

Must we anticipate? I know the Schlemihl
is the one who doesn't, the hapless one
caught with no umbrella, no special
accomplishment, no barricades, not even
the armor of a name against that time
where circumstance can crumble, history snare
the private in a public net. Some claim
it helps to understand.
                                        I beg to differ.
History is not made only from above,
not only in retrospect, not by self-fulfilled
prophecies alone...by *all* those.
                                        Love
too late dissected's like that—
                                        hapless, then old.

A Schlemihl without her histories is a ghost
making speculations fit her unripe past.

II. A Certain Freedom of Speech

« *Lying is lovely if we choose it, and is an important component of our freedom.* »

Don't tell me a flirt from the Judengasse
can't entertain a prince or hack in style.
Tell me what the fortune-teller said
last Thursday about you-know-who (more or less).

Don't tell me everything is so...indefinite,
or ask me if it's possible to love.

Tell me about the baron who had to sell
his two gold teeth to a Jew, and this-and-that.

Tell me your imaginary life
in all its detail; tell me about your passion
for strawberries or cats. Tell me another
fairy tale—thank God for them—and if

there's time, let's compare notes on suffering
(where facts matter less than a manner of speaking).

III. *In the Jägerstrasse Garret*

*« I shall never be convinced that I am a Schlemihl and a Jewess; since
in all these years and after so much thinking about it, it has not
dawned upon me, I shall never really grasp it. »*

Where it is in to be out and a talent
to be loved for a lack and for putting down
and out and out flattering the confluent
haut monde, like Countess P. who loved nothing
so much as bourgeois slumming and Countess S.
who wore men's clothes until her belly told
the truth, ambassadors and actresses,
Prince Louis Ferdinand, the unfulfilled
and self-styled, inside outsiders of all
ranks—
         here, I'll allow myself to play
their pet ignoramus, their terminal
touch-and-go case:
                         tête-à-tête manqué.

(Still, I know that gossip isn't going to save me
when the money runs out—la!—and the novelty.)

iv. *Only Introspect*

« *One is no longer a pure creature of nature, no longer a sister of silent things.* »

Where thought matters less than thinking and truths are more
remote than lies (and so much less polite),
where the beloved matters less than the loving,
introspection tends to annihilate

all but the mood focused through the giant lens
of gossip, all but the magic, all but the grief.

Where we may see the world in an emerald ring,
all future history in the glittery face
of an antique clock, where we read each other's hands
and stroke each other's lexicons with wit,

let's be friends without adjectives or
undertones, appreciate
                    the spree
introspection tends to annihilate,
with the time of day we wouldn't give each other.

v. *Pretending*

« *Only galley slaves know each other.* »

Gossip is sweaty work. One doesn't chat
all afternoon to find out what life is like.

Under the lace and golden watch chains we're
straining to keep the secrets dressed, to fake
intimate infinities... and forget.

Today let's play we're galley slaves, all oars

put in in one direction—against the wind,
against the seas, against the circular

nature of nature. Is it because we've sinned
we're chained to each other and to the drift
of tyrannies no one can understand?

It's no use, pretending. We can't undress or lift
one finger to feel another's bare survival.

We belong with no one, no fast fellow-craft.

VI. *Perfection chez Judengasse*

« *I am not like them.* »

Why do you think the snobs hobnob with me,
flatter me, honor this Jägerstrasse garret,
accept my salt for sugar in their tea?
I've caught the word *original* as it
is said of me.

I am not like the others,

not like my fat affiliations who
in ghetto'd Breslau sweat and sway at prayers.
Appalling, yes.

And I am not like you.

If the trials of our lives don't work to make us
idiosyncratic, then what are they *for*?

Can unique be less than perfect? Jewess
or not, to be perfect is to enter
the Universe.
                    To be original
you must be from nowhere, be inscrutable.

A Kind of Failure: Count Karl von Finckenstein

« *I wanted to love him into love.* »

I'd like to be a countess—
                    comprehend
the ease that sees a way to give her hand
across a crowded theater, to a more-than-friend
and person-of-the-world, to one-of-a-kind.

I could have been—
                    this count who counted for
nothing but his name made me an offer
so boring in particulars and grandeur
I made him over, and we were one, of a kind.

When a man is nothing more than a member
of moneyname nexi and one of the kind
of lovely lies that cannot comprehend

the slightest I am—
                    one of a kind not kind...
Was *I* responsible for the particular
non-committal final unwritten letter?

VIII. *At Large*

« *Dead and mute and malignant and fearful is the whole world, the whole sunlit world.* »

Yes, the beautiful world goes hand in hand
with a beautiful man. Just try to tell me
he doesn't control the weather, doesn't play
all the music there is in the world at large.

The devil's born from concentration on
one single heart; the enchantment has you living

with some one who is not there (he's saving
appearances), but in the world at large

all is apparition. Talk about all
your eggs!... baskets of breakage on my sill
spill and run.
                    Where has he gone who's real
enough to make up closeness in the world at large?

Who's real enough to make up the sun's largesse
in the face of darkness and devilish finesse?

IX. *The Last of the Romantics*

« *I must let everything pour down on me like rain without an
umbrella.* »

All romantics suppose they are the last
real ones. Friedrich G. — no exception
in loving the Exception, me — my best
drawing room know-it-all, gave feminine
reception to all my stabs at honesty.

I loved him.

                    For forty days and forty nights
the sky forgot to blink its tears away.

What it all comes down to — pathways, gates
and signposts — washed away.

                              I told him sex
to me's a trifle, no more. We might try

to be umbrellas for each other's arks...
The sky's no limit for the perfect androgyne...

Romantics! Whether they leave you high and dry
or soak you to the bone, they have their way.

x. Too True a Reflection

*« In short, as if I stood before a temple of magic—for reality receded
before my soul that was still not empty of life—a temple I can already
see swaying; its collapse is certain and it will inevitably come down on
me and everyone else. »*

Déjà vu et déjà entendu,
a person can look outside history, past
the dreams, the lies, the theories and the true
transcendentalia of gossip.
               At last
Cassandra sees that love has nothing to do
with what's real, save to grind tense present tenses
and present pain to the point of breaking through.

My pain is public knowledge. Romances
are no antidote for too much too true
reflecting.
            Cassandra with her presence
of mind plus dislocation had a clue
to chaos, intimacy with the blind
moment of losing, love.
                 It's true
I see because I simply do not see

how to be anything but glass, dark back
to the wall, dispensing smiles, feeling them... crack.

xi. In Defense of Separation

« It was a protracted murder. »

Murder should be all at once, like art;
if protracted, dilute, diffuse, prolix, spun-
out, over-pondered, maundered from the start
with no apparent finish, who can say

for sure there is an event, a real event?

Continuity annihilates
enchantment—love's or hate's; the nonchalant
execution doesn't count.

All murder
should be quick and to the quick. All actual
evenings erase the once and random word
evening mooned at noon.
In the eternal
linkages of humanity, there is
small humanity.
I disconnect

myself,
as free from self is free from all.

XII. *The Social Animal*

« *I had to treat it like a person.* »

Each makes a space of splendor in her code
of dreams; I am only a visitor in mine,
but I know the roomy palace upside-down,

    the garden inside-out.

Illuminations, servants, vistas, gaming
tables turning with all society there
I can never reach... It is as if the air

    conferred paralysis.

Only my animal would come to me—
sheepish, loving, goatish, angora, warm—
its eyes of ecstasy, its touch a charm

    it suffered all for me...

Then, the night it didn't nudge to me
as usual, I found an empty skin
between tree roots, below a festive lantern

I couldn't dream again.

XIII.   *Stopping at Nothing*

« *The dream will stop at nothing.* »

1

Unkind noon unshadowed shafts and empties
every sense on the outermost bulwark's edge
where I stand for this dream but why I do
no one knows the mob behind me yells
up to my lover now to throw me down...

Jezebel or Jesus — no one knows.

2

I kill my other love to make him well
again with kisses. I swore I'd cure us both
with knives. I'm innocent, I scream, I have not
done a thing. It's nothing that I've *done* but that
I am. I see from the corps of women corpses how

they understand what burden makes them freeze.

3

Separating, the dream
                    will stop at nothing
naked or incomprehensible:

in dreaming nothing simply stops at nothing.

xiv.   *Double Jeopardy*

« *To live doubly is lovely.* »

Prussian Junker plus unlucky Jewess—
unlikely coalition—only in
enlightened havoc could we two begin
to live in each other's lives—ambiguous
androgyny.
              I've exchanged my family's
name for "Robert," stepped out of my skin
to assimilate reality, both known
and unknown.

              M. taught me what is worthless:
dreams, heroics, illusions, money, class...

Yes, he had all those aids to nemesis
wiped out by a saving grace—melancholy.

I taught his insolent innocence to cherish
all trivials, to make them count. His early
death made sense as I lived it—double jeopardy.

NOTE: Rahel met Alexander von der Marwitz in 1809 when he was just
twenty-two and she was near forty. His aristocratic contempt for his own
class instructed hers. He advised strongly against friendship with vulgar
Varnhagen. He died several years later in battle.

xv. *Before and After*

« *When I am dead rescue the image of my soul.* »

My heart is sore from the uneven chafe
of bliss—the itemless and timeless stroke
that excludes history, that's never enough
to counteract a life that's pure bad luck.

I wonder what the image of my soul
might be—
            a constantly draining cup of tea,
a gem of the sort my father used to sell,
a bird house taken over by warring squirrels,
a fist full of fingers everything slips through...

It all runs down: just take a minute, multiply it, waste it. I've done what I can do
to reassure those who come to tea, to grief,
to chatter or to nothing.

                              Is there life
after death they ask.   *You bet.*
                              I'm living it.

xvi. *Lovely Lies*

« *I did not want to let myself be stabbed, ... I simulated, I
dissimulated, I twisted and twisted and twisted.* »

My lies make a namely knot, a gift for game
that's banal with its bane, a sort of hack-
racked hackney passion. But can you blame
me?
        Old saws and the common shipwreck
can cut or drown me out...
                              this wastes breath.

One lie that I have given you is that
I can give you (or any one) my truth.
The lie is that love is the lie that is not
false.

Love's got a dagger under its coat
for carving up the dark. The lie is that I am
satisfied with love.
I know all about
bleeding, I say, past bleeding bad blood to come.

If only my heart could empty ante-mortem...
If only I could live in my pseudonym.

XVII. *Viewing the Body*

« *Our history is nothing but the history of our illness.* »

I'd rather wear a paper crown in bedlam
than give up grief—my best possession—proof
of having had.
Still, I suppose I am
ashamed of being inconsolable;
to be healed is harder than to heal.

I scavenge in others' losses, nurse others' fears.
My soul's half junkyard, half a hospital.
Beyond repair, beyond repair—I'm happy.

I finger the central scar by which we know
we were connected, are. This thing is dead.

Ashamed, one asks, should a corpse be viewed or not?

What choice is there? Cryptic is cryptic. Say:
"Fortuity is confusion's favorite toy."

Then gobble cakes and dance in your paper hat.

xviii. *All Excluding*

« *At my "tea table"... I sit with nothing but my dictionaries.* »

How do you do and how do you define
a "trifle"? Pastry? Sex? Destiny?

No one calls here any more. The fashion
is for titles, blue eyes, flag-waving, money...

Women, philistines, Frenchmen, Jews—all are
suspect and/or excluded. I look up
"philistine." Yes, I suppose I am. I hear
you're counted French—here, have another cup—

merci merci—if ever Napoleon was
your hero. Yes, still is. The best people
are the best people. That has been, and is,
my only attitude towards war. A trifle

stale, a trifle wasted, a life that trifles
with life itself...how many lay lonely tables?

xix. *Beau Monde*

« *How loathsome it is always having to establish one's identity first.
That alone is enough to make it so repulsive to be a Jew.* »

Abroad I'm from Berlin, but in Berlin
I'm from the Judengasse. At home I am
my history's destiny. In Prague I am

what I am: an exile *par excellence.*

Varnhagen shows me there are ways to win
tickets to *bon ton* and glitter. One who is
adept at vogue and vagueness, letters and liaison,
can mingle at Teplitz with the arty bunch.

Now: married, baptized, renamed, I've arrived
at the masquerade, to stand on what's beneath
me now, that simply can't can't simply be.

I'm from Berlin, the Judengasse, planet Earth.

Don't get me wrong—I'm grateful for a crown,
even if I have to wear it upside-down.

xx. *Abstract*

« *The poverty of the city where I can calculate what everyone has,*
consumes, wants, or can do: the frightful, vacuous unrelatedness,
looking neither to love, family, or any kind of self-created religion.
Their dizzying, vain, trivial, criminally repulsive chaos. I among
them, still more unrelated... separated from the ultimate. »

I must be careful. Alien is not
necessarily superior;
to get the large view you must separate
yourself, make maxims of moon-dust, despair

the desireless way, the only real despair,
recognized by the fact you are ashamed
and disconnected from its source. The poor
in spirit lack natural ties, are damned

for dumb illusions and moral scruples—none
of which I share. The rich in spirit cult-
ivate some truth...
                    but since when has truth been human?

Am I the sum of ghosts, the difficult
one plus one that yields a minus one?
The truth is careless.
                    The truth I leave alone.

xxi. *Beggar by the Wayside: Varnhagen*

« *I have a young husband who loves me dearly. There is nothing
more comical. The upside-down crown upon my fate; still I am
grateful.* »

The empty soul is a beggar and borrower.
It waits.
            The never-entangled wayside watcher
absorbs my life in detail. He is like nothing so much as a jellyfish:
                        see-through,
reflective and vague, unsinkable and free.

I become his curiosity,
his mine of anecdotes;
                my diary
improves his atmosphere, my utterance
his lukewarm sentiments.
                    Evasive, numb,
the Prime Unknown, the void, but real as rain
and good as gold—at least he's more than the sum
of his happiness and his unhappiness.

There is great potential in emptiness,
rainbows in the simplest jellyfish.

xxii. *Pariah Parvenu*

« *I can swear to Almighty God that never in my life have I overcome
a weakness.* »

Born exiled it is hard to break the habit
of living the impossible living lack
of certainties, connections....
                    so you marry,
change your name, faith, station; try dividing

nothing into nothing much. It goes,
too many times, it goes...

You try to fit
in somewhere and mask the weaknesses that give
the game away, like excess gratitude—
the outcast's kneejerk thanks, or sympathy—
that old corset. (Involuntary
morality is shaped by it.)

I blush
at things "real" people never need or show,
a morbid sense of dignity in chains
of mishap.

Pariah values, unrenovated fate.

XXIII. *Exemplary*

« *Let me have suffered for you.* »

Is the whole meaning of history to make
examples, extracts, abstracts, essences...?
rules to die by once you find you're sick
of endless idiosyncrasies? Or is

the whole meaning of history to explain
the need for explanations—obvious
chaos overlaid with fragile chains
of "events" (they say) that lead somewhere—to this:

the whole meaning of history is to prepare
the outcast to be clairvoyant. Look at me!
Did you ever see so disorganized
a genius for suffering, or realize
such a gift for abstracting it? Is there
a purpose? If none, still, I can be...

xxiv. *A Changed Person*

« *I could not have done anything differently.* »

Forgetting—my favorite of life forces—
makes me fear reiteration less
where we begin and end, begin and end:

> *a name can be a blessing or a curse.*

Identities in deshabille, we think
we have a choice. We do. A drop of water,
mumbo-jumbo, a wedding ring, and Rahel
steps out:
> *Antonie Friederike Robert Varnhagen von Ense.*

Goethe once called on a person of that name.

I wasn't dressed. I fastened on my black
work skirt. I shook. I shook his hand. The chosen
one can't ask the center of the universe
to wait.

> When the great man left I changed to white
with lace.
> *I had a rite to celebrate.*

xxv. *Far and Dear*

« I rejoice, banished as I was by those near and dear to me, without fortune, rank, youth, name, talents, to see that I can nevertheless find my place in the world. »

I am this person. So people come for tea.
I might be that person. (I might not.)
There is infinite possibility
in parentheticality.   Forget

if possible, my misfortune's fiction:
in fact there is no fact that cannot be
denied. Yet the world's a blur I can't begin
to contradict in detail, lie by lie.

I never was struck down by destiny
and suffer from the fact I never suffered

to be this person.
                    Curiosity
is a sort of magnet.
                    People come. They've heard...

I might be this odd person, or what   .
can't believe I can believe I might
as well be...
                    the Levy girl sweetening lemon tea.

xxvi. *The Living Ends*

« At the end of things it is good again — like everything, when we understand it. »

I

We must end sometime. Incompletion is
not freedom. Once you start to dance the fan-

dango you're committed — awkwardness
in the middle's no excuse for sitting down.

I lived all the fumbling and juggling out
and down to the last embarrassments and shame.
Now, near the end, I'm free again to write
my brother with Hebrew characters. I am

moving backwards, like the world — so fast
that if I don't die soon I'll meet Lot's wife
in the pantry, Sarah in bed, Eve bushed
in the back yard. It's been a trying life —

the first society, always. So back to Lilith —
flings and funks — the ends to begin with...

2

So this is what life is like. You pour yourself
into all ears and eavesdrop on the sphinx.

What odd shapes wisdom comes in. Out of
daily life, lies, mute laments...
                              you think
only happiness or death can open your
Pandora's box, let hope complete the mess.

Fate uses men and women like mother nature
uses dead things, for living ends.
                              The past —

that crystal ball of balls — there is
no future futures in it — that I can see.

O, I can see it now — after all these
years of aversion, years of lamenting my
history:
            it is not one's being understood
but understanding that can make it — good.

WOMAN WITH QUASAR

*an essay in honor of the birthday of
the universe, certain loving beings,
and the unlikelihood of all of it*

I. *Her frame of reverence*

A woman with all most
                              anything is easier
posing for a portrait
                              than a woman alone
as this one is
with the quasi-stellar object
                              of her desire
as none surpasses the obscurity
                              of one and none
surpasses
the brilliance of the other
                              as both are either
blinding by want or by glut
                              of light—all in—
explicable—neither
one nor the other—exclusively—
                              yet coming closer
still—nothing in between... is there
                              nothing between
the two then? Star
or no star, framed by wonder
                              she is so far
confused with what she holds
                              so close, no one
can ask too much
about her. Feeling she is missing
                              a part of the picture
(having focused on the big one)
                              so far and away, she's chosen
her quasar over such
props as beau, fan, lute
                              tiger-skin or flower
gallantries and illusions
                              touching a vision
so remote, she is
like the first one in the garden
                              asking for more

than has ever been given
                              and gnawing forbidden
transitions—yes—
and resonant ones, feeding surplus
                              to her computer.
Where the background is very faint
                              we know... it's known
to swallow any
small hard fact can make the missing
                              less intense for
a time being. See how demure
                    she is—to put on
that tastefully
basic black with pearls
                    to emphasize the nature
of her formal study. Quasi-true
                    or quasi-fiction
is neither here nor
there to come to her co-star so far
                              unproven and so far
from reason (or any given) some say
                              it's not even
real, that there
is nothing in her big picture but
                    a pretense—her
rich dress and Nobel glance with
                    "where is the crown?"
All of this here
is speculation you understand.
                    Can love ever
be neither here nor there? now and then at once?
                                        We question
her quasar.

II. *What might make a lady sphinx herself*

What might make a lady study
    the one impossible fabric of space
What might make a stellar lady
    play opposite an unknown knock-about
What might make her make a quasi-
    star the one true falsehood of her time

1 for the money

    that the swivelings of her eye surveys
    her fortune to make it a whole
    and rich philosophy

2 for the show

    that in time has shown her the false
    muff and burley-q and headline hunter
    to be honester about the universe
    than any answer

3 to get ready

    for the language of stone and mistrust
    defines a trust in things that are
    in variable dimensions just

4 to go

    for even if she's no lady after
    all or after nothing and no sphinx either
    she will have been how ever peculiar
    now forever

III. *In her slantingdicular position*

She is not crouched like a snail-cuckoo
  in the trunk of the Palomar telescope
    slaunchwise, her aura exceptionally
      blue, for nothing—
        oh no—but for the asking

she has got her camera to color by number
  has got her finger pressed to the pressing pulse
    has got some graphs in a rat's nest of chance
      and in her pink
        she has got more than any one

pulling off red shift after shift after shift,
  biting into the apple with the unresolved core,
    tasting ultraviolet excesses, putting a tail on
      the whole sky lit up by her wish
        for her asking to one with one.

IV. *Daring her darling a personal note*

A woman with a quasar—
forbidding.
Do I dare address her?
Try. Woman,

you try me. My eyes' blood
rips through you
like electrical syrup
equally good

for loving or killing
giant mass
or tiny tissue. I
try you on

many charges: for sheer
size, a change
of heart... My god—she's made
out of light.

Me too. She is. You are.
Out of sight.
Woman, you try me on
all so—so

I sing like Galileo
marking secs
with syllables, and woe-

man, I dare you dare you
dare you dare...

you too care.

v. *One to worry if a love has many: reasons and explications in the event of her*

(1)

There is only one reason for them
to be together: they find each other
accidentally sharing some finite space.

Why did someone make their image or
measure corner to corner to frame
this awful asymmetry?

Never mind. Let both framed and framers
be, as kangaroos in some pre-
discovered Antartica, anonymous.

Otherwise there are too many.

(2)

Purely and absolutely. What we want
to know is no blasphemy.
But does her quasar signify

a beginning or an end? There are,
we suppose, the same possibilities
for her as for her object

with which you see her arranging
herself and posing and playing darts...
Can picture and question be

synonymous? To some proposals then:
1) she may not exist at all or
2) be falsely meaningful

at her own—astronomical of course—
expense—putting out to be putting out or
3) she may have been herself put out

by a central angry matrix, but no...
she is simply too bright to have slipped
or spilled from a milky rib.

A proposal is either beginning or ending.

(3)

Marrow cannot outshine the heart
(ah, what a start!) it leaves behind.
The cage is not more mysterious

than the animal it frees. 4) She—maybe—
is the most discrepant bird in the world
for all we know as the reasons in her

wings get longer as we seem to look
at her conceptions. The quasar is this
sort of event—in the mere twinkling of

her eye. To observe certain laws
while she hangs there like a jury
or green herring on the wall

is tiresome. Follow her verdictless scent
to the hoosegow then, my friend,
or to the rose garden...

where some few find themselves.

VI. *A crying matter*

The sky. *The sky is just so much*
noise, she cries.
So far. *So far we have plotted*

a ratio of
every fat chance to all, so long
divided

this body and that—every one
that might make
clear the difference between the

center and
edges. We have subtracted the
human and

inhuman interferences
multiplied,
added in speed of light, she cries,

and until,
an occurrence appearing to
emerge, the

ultimate collapse is at her
fingertips
in-quasi-venting super-stars

all of one
piece with vision and honor, she
cries. So much.

So much for a single body
to bear so
many—so many energies.

Too much, she
cries, *for the cause of difference*
between the

absorption and emission, in
lines illum-
inating nothing but no light

and dark itself at the center.
She cries, throws
her light around, this way and that,

as if it
were given, and not just to her,
that light is

heavy and enough to make a
difference
between every thing—festival

and murder,
old and new—and we are just
beginning

to know there
is a fuel to feel for in her
cries beyond

register.

VII.   *Heavy cat where gravity flips (not quite a laughing matter)*

(T
his on
e may not
be appropria
te.) / A cat's pa
w on the edge / of t
he visible in her daydre
ams / she whispers & strok
es one platinum / pulsed angor
a shape in her lap, / transfers azur
e to earth. (Perhaps it's / not appropri
ate.) Between cat ears / sensing the feline
totem's token/unseen deep past scarlet, she t
aps a lost eye. / (This may not be appropriate.)/
A purr comes from a core so uranium dense/(and p
roperly inappropriate)/ all light willows, & loves to/c
at's curve, magnifies moving / close, casts its shifting nihilis
tic eye up / on a power of pyramid gravity./Her delta swells o
ver fields of prayer/(appropriately)/as bitter far sweet urges near.

(This one may not be appropriate.)
A cat's paw on the edge
of the visible in her daydreams
she whispers & strokes one platinum
pulsed angora shape in her lap,
transfers azure to earth. (Perhaps it's
not appropriate.) Between cat ears
sensing the feline totem's token
unseen deep past scarlet, she taps a lost eye.
(This may not be appropriate.)
A purr comes from a core so uranium dense
(and properly inappropriate)
all light willows, and loves to
cat's curve, magnifies moving
close, casts its shifting nihilistic eye up
on a power of pyramid gravity.
Her delta swells over fields of prayer
(appropriately)
as bitter far sweet urges near.

VIII.   *Or the flight of the bumblebee*

Impossible.
            Take the flight of
the bumblebee—it's
aerodynamically
impossible.
            And the light of
this huddled-in-fuzz-
buzzing-off thing is just as
                                    quasi-
impossible.

        Like that other, Love.
        Tra la. Like that.

Violations.
            Give tickets for
speeding—light traffic
is no excuse, nor lost time—
violations.
            And tablets for
feeling motion sick
of the divine are comic:
                                    quasi-
violations.

        Like that other, Fear.
        Tra la. Like that.

The quasar, love, paid
no attention to its own impossibility.

The quasar, love, received
no ovations for its being violated.

The quasar, love, is the flight
of the bumblebee, the ticket to the limit.

Take it.
For what she is.
Take it from there.
For what she may be.

IX. *A terminal case: dancing the dying light*

Presenting symptoms: suffocation and desire
to leave certain premises behind for those
less/more/less/more so.

Appearance: mysterious, the accidental
Isadorian scarf and classic mode
of barely breathing

yet races past sense—"*Adieu, mes amis,
je vais à la gloire*"—last words the specter
of simplicity.

Another says, "I guess I'll just go Southwest
for a little sun," meaning to meet you in the woods
before long after all.

Disappearance: unexpected in your dream she flirts
around the corner of the gingerbread cottage
in a red pinafore,

dashes over the stream of stars, flauntering
good-byes as quick as light graphing leaves
you alone sleeping there.

For her to escape you that way she must share
some of your beaten blood. Woman or quasar—
now—or neither—then.

Departing symptoms: in sum fashion: settled in her vehicle,
your gentle nightmare her auto, she's a trillion times brighter
than an Arizona noon.

x. *Not unlike a postscript to the universe*

The body scribbled out star by wise star
    (the salutation merely formal
      the signature immaterial),
she focuses on the postscript where things are
god's afterthoughts.

No gospel epistle can be complete
    (the salutation to a body unknown
      the signature ash in an urn)
without the coda she cannot penetrate
stellar tails, pieces.

Here on earth she studies its strange hand
    (the salutation stiff with nerves
      the signature throwing its curves)
and the postscript—a stroke of luck—a penned
luxury without end.

xi. *Selling the big picture*

Ladies and Gentlemen—introducing
    the Q-ish keeno going
thing as good as all get-
    out & out A-double-1
rare-o flash & foxy
    from way back passing
in the dark your dazzling
    daubs for sure she's monstrous fine

as scrum & yet plum of
    a heaven's high-tone spiff
bright as the devil's cuff-
    links—bang-up & royal flush

honey humdinger
    alagazam & very hot stuff
so step right up for
    dreamducks & rose meows too precious

for words: from the bee's
    knees to the mosquito's
eyebrows & oyster's ice
    skates to snake's toenails
a woman with a quasar
    is one brilliant cat's pajamas
of a catch—who sleeps with her
    sleeps where no star falls.

XII. *The domino theory: mock saccharine's real snow*

    (1)

and gravity also
    has a highly artificial character
loving equally

regardless of mass—no
    lightning no magnet no friction no other
force can fall this way

and too good to be true—
    her feet on its ground one cannot deprive her
sticky quality

    (2)

or her dream in blue
    coming closer, the quasar's nothing other
(her discovery)

than spun sugar, so
    sweet it heats her tongue, frizzes all angel hair
to cotton candy

(1)

don't ask me
of all things
how do I know
all I know is

(2)

as someone else has poignantly remarked.

$$\frac{ds}{dt} = 3At^2 + B.$$

seems to be so not-I.

and may it be as graphic as you like.

(3)

just as long as.

art.
life.

remember it is always positive.

(4)

(thanks to the imaginary operator)
$$i$$
(when this thou see remember her)

(5)

there will always be time.
four a manifold.
a cozy of corners.

(6)

centrifugal force is a fiction, dear.
and gravity, love, has no antagonist.
save wishing well well wishing saves.
which is to say.
she is not trying to escape any thing.

(7)

simply moving on.
don't ask.
as someone not-I has.
life.
i's manifold.
goodness.
to be in any.
art.
a personal thing.

(8)

at the still point, though.
there is.
coming back to it.
all I know.

(9)

and it shall be given.
to ask.

xiv. *Taking them asterisks and hanging together*

them stars notes the saltsmear astronomers
is god's open litter to the universifiers
in bold type—comets and tortoised meremyths
all so and all those who ain't in other whirls
much literate can read tho'

                        not necessarily...

but them's the piths

and them quasi-ones many is—is queasy after all
them supernotions rock their boats—plode whole
galaxies of gall—where not all flows with milks
and—honeys—it's proven proof—against the still
dots trips the light fantastic toe

                        not necessarily...

but them's the tricks

and them asides whisks dé tours et ceteras are
ad libs twixting ignomighters and their cinders
to hide one who bundles up good big mistakes
in margins as if they weren't no matters
much like postscripts to put the touch to

                        necessarily...

but them's the aches

in the dark man and matters womanlikes
is in the know no—how irrelevants—

                    and them's the real sin tax.

xv. *Her X mass our primavera passion gliding*

(1)

Strange pietà—a telescope
resting cold on her more hot thighs—
all the distance in those dark tubes
the world runs through like light.

Someone draws this up or down,
hangs it, mounts it, the trophy of a trial.
She holds hers in her lap, a symbol of all
the big fish stories, and hers beats all

hollow. Her telescope and her eyes
go blind in the solar masses passed
through them; she seems to be living
nevertheless in the very saint nick

of time with its sack of gaudy presents.
And in all her born days never you mind
her P's and Q's, her pulses and little quavers
conceiving to bear what's over and above.

The quasi-star points the way to another
truth and light. She's one curvaceous
madonna, space, enfolding such generous
waste—light years of Sabbaths in nothing

flat, her matter responsible for
the space left behind, between us, increasing, increasing...
More strange pietà, as if blown glass
transparent as tears, surface magnifying

the moon and all—an intensest goldfish
having swallowed the pearl without
its price (of an image) or the brag of heaven's
ocean—coming it all over—eelight.

Slouched in the final musical chair
in the wake of the last and only speed
boat we know, she reels and reels in — her line
the quasar's loss and the concert's gain

from humming tops. Believing in her catch
as the brightest barracuda of all essences
invisible, she reels its violence in
response to nothing but the possible body

tugging at the end of her line.
She reels with the weight of it,
sways in the spray of it finally landing
the darkness in her hook's bare prong

and lightness in the frame upon her frame.

XVI.   *Negative capability: a quasarisky business*

As art, her business is heavy
        departures—
blood-red—but knowing Certainty
and Triviality—mighty
        dull lovers,

she can bear not knowing—knowing
        the finite
to be mystery minus nothing,
or N.C.: 'nuff ced, no craving,
        no credit...

"It is better to travel hope-
        fully than
to arrive"—a Confucian quip
that rattles round her telescope.
        It's human

nature to believe. She is grate-
        ful to some
ends: the speed of light—to let
her see her love's past: not complete
        in no time.

DATE DUE

MOORE READING ROOM
KU RELIGIOUS STUDIES DEPARTMENT
109 SMITH HALL
LAWRENCE, KANSAS